MW00411990

"By the obvious lead... ... ...g personal testimony and Scriptural insight, Zeke Lam in *SUBMISSION*, captures the essence of true spiritual revival and growth: complete surrender and submission to the Will and Word of God. In our world of political correctness, warped ideologies and confused beliefs, where submission is equated to weakness, *SUBMISSION* will exhort you to discover the power of a surrendered life, and challenge and inspire you to live in the joy and blessings of a life yielded to the Father."

—JIM AND JOANNA FAILLACE
Evangelists, Songwriters/Musicians

"In his book *SUBMISSION*, Zeke Lam challenges each of us to take an honest look at our hearts and question whose mission we're really after. Prepare to be stirred by this authentic calling to return to Scriptural obedience."

—GABE TURNER, PASTOR
The Point Church of Charlottesville, Virginia

"*SUBMISSION* is a must read for any Christian who desires to come back to their first love, Jesus Christ. This book is anointed, powerful, and convicting. I pray that we all learn what it is to humbly come back to the heart of God as is so powerfully displayed in this book."

—ADAM MEISBERGER, PASTOR
Bethel Baptist Church in Reva, Virginia

"Zeke Lam is a common man with uncommon characteristics. He has the ability to authoritatively communicate divine principles with disarming humility. His knowledge of the Word and love for the will of God are both challenging and inspiring. Lastly, the principles taught in his book are readily seen in his life."

—ERIC STEPHENS AND MATTHEW PEROT, PASTORS
Life Changing Ministries in Sugarland, Texas

subMISSION

HEEDING ONLY HIS VOICE

sub**MISSION**

HEEDING ONLY HIS VOICE

ZEKE LAM

BURNING LAMP™
media & publishing

SUB**MISSION** by: Zeke Lam
Published by BURNING LAMP MEDIA & PUBLISHING
An Imprint of DOMINION LEADERSHIP SOLUTIONS
P.O. Box 1284
Haymarket, VA 20168
www.burninglampmap.com

Cover Design: Anthony Antenucci of Zakr Studios
Interior Design: Gabriel Leonhard of Voyage Media Group
Printed in the United States of America
First Edition 2011

CONTENTS

FOREWORD

I remember during my college years as the Lord was drawing me closer to Himself, I continually prayed one prayer in particular, "God, I wonder what you could do through just one person who is completely, fully, and wholly surrendered and submitted to You above all things."

I was so frustrated with mediocre Christianity. I had noticed many confessing Christians who, when they were in a prayer gathering or Bible study, seemed so on fire for God but in the everyday routine of life many of those same Christians often said and did things that did not reflect a person on fire for God. I can recall the feeling of anger that burned within me over this hypocrisy.

However, as the Lord always does, He began to turn my attention away from pointing my fingers and began to set my eyes toward myself. I started to realize that in my own life there were areas that did not reflect a man fully submitted to the Lord. I became frustrated with my own weaknesses, my own struggles, and my own lack of surrender. I longed for more of Jesus Christ and less of me. I desired Jesus to fully take over my life and make me into the man that He wanted me to be. And so began the ongoing journey of what I call "learned submission."

From my early college years to the present, the Lord has been constantly teaching me how to submit everything to Him. And trust me; I do not have it all together just yet. I am still learning. That is the key, learning. As we go through this journey of life, we are constantly learning how to submit all things to Christ. We are maturing. A baby doesn't grow up over night, but over time that baby becomes a toddler, and then a child, and then a teenager, and then an adult.

As I recall the words that I prayed during my college years about being fully submitted to God, one thing I didn't take into consideration was this idea of "learned submission." In Philippians 3:12, the apostle Paul writes, "...continue to work out your salvation in fear and trembling." Our Christian walk to maturity takes time. Submitting to the Lord is a learned process.

My wife and I have been blessed with three beautiful children. I thank God every day for each of them; yet, I have realized something as a dad: children do not have a lot of patience. One particular summer day, my wife and I loaded our kids into the van and headed to a public water park. The water park was close to an hour away, and our oldest son, who is four years old, complained the whole way there: "It is too far away! ... Are we there yet? ...Why is it so far?!!" My wife and I constantly told him that we would be there when we got there and that we couldn't help that the water park was so far away.

I wonder how many times we Christians treat our journey with Christ in a similar way. In our minds and hearts, we see the person that we want to be, but we want to be that person now. We don't want to wait. We want the water park without the long drive to get there. We want the trophy without having to run the long and exhausting race. We want to be a person fully submitted to Christ without the struggles of having to slowly learn how to become that person.

I believe Jesus is saying to us, "I want to teach you *how to become* a person fully submitted to Me." The journey may not be an easy one, but as we continue to abide in Christ on a daily basis, the Lord will teach us how to be a servant truly submitted to Him. We must persevere because the more we learn to submit to Christ, the more we will understand that we can trust Him, and the more we will come to the realization of just how great His love and faithfulness truly are toward us who believe.

In this book, *SUBMISSION*, Zeke Lam wonderfully and simply explains what it is to be completely surrendered to God. As Christians, we often say that we want to be a people fully submitted to Him, but many of us do not understand what this type of life looks like. This book will reveal to you in a very clear and straightforward manner what a life of submission to God looks like and how **you** can become that person.

Zeke Lam has been a close friend of mine for some time now, and I know he is a man who desires to be completely submitted before Jesus Christ above all things. Zeke is one who desires to please God by doing His will and by walking in obedience to His Word. I have not met many men who are as humble and real as Zeke.

In this book are the words of a man who truly loves God and desperately desires to submit every area of his life to Him. You will be blessed by Zeke's words. I can assure you that through the reading of this book, you will draw closer to the heart of God, and you will be greatly encouraged and motivated to be a person who daily lives the life of submission to Him.

—ADAM MEISBERGER
Pastor of Bethel Baptist Church, Reva, Virginia

SCRIPTURE
Start Here!

As we journey through this book towards a life fully submitted to the Lord Jesus, I want to present a framework from a story concerning Saul. Please commit your heart to the reading of this opening passage of Scripture. The theme of this book is illustrated to perfection as the plot of this story unfolds before your very eyes. Before we dissect God's message to His people concerning true submission and obedience, allow me to explain why this passage identifies with this particular book so accurately.

God's Word is alive and well within the lives of those who choose to follow His voice. We have the unique privilege of hearing and receiving His word through the Scriptures and experiencing intimacy with Him.

Something has happened within the Body of Christ that has proven to be a spiritual devastation. Slowly and ever so subtly, man has intertwined human ideologies with the word of the Lord and ultimately contaminated what should be perfection. From matters relating to spiritual gifts and eternal security, to everyday concerns such as forgiveness and purity, humanistic philosophies have watered down the authentic truth recorded in the Bible. Although it is not the intent of this book to dissect those specific issues, it is the desire of *SUBMISSION* to illuminate the importance and power of living a life yielded **solely** to the voice of the Lord.

The moment we seek to incorporate our thoughts and opinions with the pure truth of God's Word, we step into a realm of disobedience that will cost us dearly. This can clearly be seen in the life of Saul as recorded in I Samuel 15:

> Samuel also said to Saul, "The LORD sent me to anoint you king over His people, over Israel. Now therefore, heed the voice of the words of the LORD. [2]Thus says the LORD of hosts: 'I will punish Amalek for what he did to Israel, how he ambushed him on the way when he came up from Egypt. [3]Now go and attack Amalek, and utterly destroy all that they have, and do not spare them. But kill both man and woman, infant and nursing child, ox and sheep, camel and donkey.'" [4]So Saul gathered the people together and numbered them in Telaim, two hundred thousand foot soldiers and ten thousand men of Judah. [5]And Saul came to a city of Amalek and lay

in wait in the valley. [6]Then Saul said to the Kenites, "Go, depart, get down from among the Amalekites, lest I destroy you with them. For you showed kindness to all the children of Israel when they came up out of Egypt." So the Kenites departed from among the Amalekites. [7]And Saul attacked the Amalekites, from Havilah all the way to Shur, which is east of Egypt. [8]He also took Agag king of the Amalekites alive, and utterly destroyed all the people with the edge of the sword. [9]But Saul and the people spared Agag and the best of the sheep, the oxen, the fatlings, the lambs, and all that was good, and were unwilling to utterly destroy them. But everything despised and worthless, that they utterly destroyed. [10]Now the word of the LORD came to Samuel, saying, [11]"I greatly regret that I have set up Saul as king, for he has turned back from following Me, and has not performed My commandments." And it grieved Samuel, and he cried out to the LORD all night.

[12] So when Samuel rose early in the morning to meet Saul, it was told Samuel, saying, "Saul went to Carmel, and indeed, he set up a monument for himself; and he has gone on around, passed by, and gone down to Gilgal." [13]Then Samuel went to Saul, and Saul said to him, "Blessed are you of the LORD! I have performed the commandment of the LORD." [14]But Samuel said, "What then is this bleating of the sheep in my ears, and the lowing of the oxen which I hear?" [15]And Saul said, "They have brought them

from the Amalekites; for the people spared the best of the sheep and the oxen, to sacrifice to the LORD your God; and the rest we have utterly destroyed." [16]Then Samuel said to Saul, "Be quiet! And I will tell you what the LORD said to me last night." And he said to him, "Speak on." [17]So Samuel said, "When you were little in your own eyes, were you not head of the tribes of Israel? And did not the LORD anoint you king over Israel? [18]Now the LORD sent you on a mission, and said, 'Go, and utterly destroy the sinners, the Amalekites, and fight against them until they are consumed.' [19]Why then did you not obey the voice of the LORD? Why did you swoop down on the spoil, and do evil in the sight of the LORD?" [20]And Saul said to Samuel, "But I have obeyed the voice of the LORD, and gone on the mission on which the LORD sent me, and brought back Agag king of Amalek; I have utterly destroyed the Amalekites. [21]But the people took of the plunder, sheep and oxen, the best of the things which should have been utterly destroyed, to sacrifice to the LORD your God in Gilgal." [22]So Samuel said: "Has the LORD as great delight in burnt offerings and sacrifices, as in obeying the voice of the LORD? Behold, to obey is better than sacrifice, And to heed than the fat of rams. [23]For rebellion is as the sin of witchcraft, And stubbornness is as iniquity and idolatry. Because you have rejected the word of the LORD, He also has rejected you from being king."

—1 Samuel 15:1-23

God is not concerned with our opinions. He is not con-cerned with our various theological reasoning and meth-odologies. He is concerned with one thing and one thing alone. Will we, as His children, be obedient and submissive to His voice only? The importance of achieving this goal is simply this: only within the humble act of full surrender will we position ourselves in the perfect will of God. It is there that we walk

> WE ARE TAKING THE WORD OF GOD, MIXING IT WITH A LOT OF MAN, AND CALLING IT OBEDIENCE.

in freedom and power to live daily the Christian life that is promised us. Pursuing our desires with no regard for Christ will leave us empty and broken every time. Under Him, how-ever, is a fulfillment and satisfaction unattainable through any other source.

The title of this book is *SUBMISSION* because it is my heart's desire to illustrate that when followers of Christ ren-der fully to the commands and ways of the Lord, widespread revival **will** occur!

Why are we witnessing a falling away within the walls of this country? God's people are not operating under full submission. We are taking the Word of God, mixing it with a lot of man, and calling it obedience. This is dead wrong and the exact mentality that is restricting the flow of revival to this nation.

I want to point out four specific verses within this passage of I Samuel 15 that will prepare us for the message of this book. My prayer is that you will earnestly seek to see your heart forever changed for the glory of the Lord.

> ➢ God's words to Saul: destroy **ALL** (I Samuel 15:3).

> ➢ Saul **spares** Agag and the best animals (I Samuel 15:8-9).

> ➢ Saul **thinks** he obeyed the word of the Lord (I Samuel 15:13).

I Samuel 15:3 clearly reveals how God instructed Saul to destroy all. Saul thought it would be fitting to save the very best that he might offer a sacrifice before the Lord. At first glance, that may seem to be an innocent intent of the heart. One problem: it was not the command of the Lord. It was a **part** of the command combined with an **ideology** of man. Ultimately, it proved to be purely disgusting in the Lord's sight. Why? God is not interested in our opinions or what we have to offer to Him. He wants our obedience, and that is the only thing that you and I possess worthy to be presented before the Lord.

> HE WANTS OUR OBEDIENCE, AND THAT IS THE ONLY THING THAT YOU AND I POSSESS WORTHY TO BE PRESENTED BEFORE THE LORD.

I Samuel 15:8-9 offers a vivid description of disobedience. God gave a simple command. Somehow, Saul was under the impression that his advice would assist God's command. This is a classic example of an ideology of man seeking communion with the plan of the Lord. This is wrong; this is sin and the very recipe for disaster!

I Samuel 15:13 follows with a powerful truth we must understand as we seek to hear from the Lord concerning submission. Read Saul's response to Samuel in verse 13. I call this denial or self deception. He actually **thinks** he heeded the voice of the Lord. Partial obedience is disobedience any way you look at it.

This is our problem, brothers and sisters. This kind of erroneous thinking has infected our homes, our churches, our universities, and our hearts. Simply stated, the actions such as those demonstrated by Saul are not submission but rather idolatry.

Anything that stands between you and Jesus is an idol. Therefore, anything that stands between you and obeying His voice is an idol. Idolatry is not limited to images, cults, or statues. Rather, it is a condition of the heart that separates you from fellowship with Him. Submission is about identifying those areas of your life which block communion with the Lord and removing them. In doing this, you surrender your will to His and position yourself for victory.

Saul's idol happened to be his opinion. That is a very relevant issue today. Walking a submitted life will require us to release our opinions and focus on obeying God's voice. Placing our own desires and opinions in the place of His is **idolatry!** (Note: If the Lord's command to Saul sounds harsh

to you, please take time here to read what the Amalekites did
to the children of God in Exodus 17.)

This passage is saturated with powerful truth, but we will
not elaborate further. God wants us, as we begin to understand true submission, to remove the blinders of self deception and be honest with our hearts. The very moment we
move past our thoughts and desires and opinions and step
into the realm of full submission to the voice of the Lord,
revival will begin.

As you begin reading this book, I want to make one point
very clear. It is all about submitting to the Lord's voice:
Nothing more, nothing less. If you desire to see revival personally, nationally, and globally, remove your thoughts and
ideas and obey His Word.

Obedience is better than sacrifice.

So Samuel said: "Has the Lord as great
delight in burnt offerings and sacrifices, as
in obeying the voice of the Lord? Behold,
to obey is better than sacrifice, And to heed
than the fat of rams."

—I Samuel 15:22

INTRODUCTION
Relinquish the Grave Clothes

W e had no idea what to expect as we approached the house. Trees had surrounded us, providing a great escape from the sun as we'd walked through the village distributing supplies and offering the love of Christ through prayer. I can vividly remember walking into the muddy courtyard before entering the home. Several scrawny animals scurried about our feet as we listened to the mother of the house interact with our missionary and translator.

Although I could not clearly discern their dialogue, my instincts sensed a significant urgency in the lady's voice. She quickly directed us through the yard and the kitchen area. As we turned the corner of the dark and humid house, my eyes caught a glimpse of a sight that radically altered my relationship with Christ.

Before I explain our encounter that day, let me ask you a question. Have you ever heard the phrase "beaten into submission"? That term often passed my ears growing up, and although I never fully understood it as a youth, it became clearer as I matured. The word submission implies the act of yielding or relinquishing control to someone or something. Therefore, if I were beaten into submission, I would have experienced a yielding of my control at the expense of some sort of physical strength, power, or even an illness.

Often in sports which involve hand to hand combat, such as boxing, the word submission is rather familiar. When a competitor submits, he or she relinquishes the match to the opponent. In simple terms, submission is the act of being under the full control of something or someone.

In this small Honduran hut, God was about to illustrate "beaten into submission" in a way I had never experienced it in my Christian walk. I and four others rounded the corner and entered the gloomy and clammy bedroom area. Lying on a hard cot on a dirt floor and wrapped in a tattered wool blanket was a young man beaten into submission. Sweat poured from his brow. He shook like a leaf on a tree as he curled into a fetal-like position. As we approached his bed, we felt heat radiating from his body. Having contracted a severe form of malaria, this young man was experiencing submission in a most unusual way. Physically speaking, he could not function. All his power had been momentarily relinquished to the illness.

While this may not immediately appear like submission, please consider the definition for a moment. Despite his desire to arise and continue with his life, this teenage boy lay yielded to the sickness. He could not work. He could not talk. He could not even open his eyes because the illness had robbed him of any and all energy his body had possessed. In that moment, he was yielded completely to the power of that sickness in his life.

> IN SIMPLE TERMS, SUBMISSION IS THE ACT OF BEING UNDER THE FULL CONTROL OF SOMETHING OR SOMEONE.

Although it is a peculiar way to teach a lesson, God's message appears clearly. The question to analyze is simply this: what if I allow that level of submission to reign in my life with Christ? What if I speak only what He allows me to speak? What if I only go where He sends me? That level of submission would significantly alter my life. When God's children yield and relinquish all authority to the Lord, they begin a Christ-like walk capable of miracles and revival.

Being fully submitted to the malaria, the young Honduran brother did things typically associated with that condition. He sweated profusely with fever. He shook uncontrollably. He panted and labored hard to breathe. The illness dominated and characterized his life.

Being fully submitted to Christ, we would operate in a

fashion associated with Him. **Every** area of our lives would be characterized by that of the Lord Jesus Christ. Based on the testimony of the Word of God, I would say He is an incredible authority to be yielded to.

Opening Thoughts

In a humble confession, I proclaim that I know very little about God's specific intentions for you as you read the words of this book. This journal, with its empty pages, rested on my nightstand for at least a year. God often requires acts from His servants that they may not necessarily be accustomed to. His selection of me to pen these words certainly fits such a description.

It is my heart's desire that the presence of the Lord will flood your life as you seek to draw closer to the Savior. May He use these words to charge and urge those of us in the Body of Christ to **arise** and prepare our hearts for obedience. IT IS TIME! Soften the hearts of your people Lord, and allow us to hear only Your voice.

> For He is our God, And we are the people of His pasture, And the sheep of His hand. Today, if you will hear His voice: "Do not harden your hearts, as in the rebellion, as in the day of trial in the wilderness."
>
> —Psalm 95: 7-8

Relinquish the Grave Clothes

When people commit a crime and are detained, what is the

first thing that happens to them? Depending on the severity of the offense, they are possibly handcuffed and jailed and become the possession of the government. The purpose for that binding is to restrict their freedom and hold them captive, that they may receive the due compensation for their crime.

Clearly, this is a legitimate process and a critical need in order to assure protection among the civilians. Not a person reading these words would probably object or deny the importance of such law enforcement. An individual who presents himself as a threat to the safety of this society must be bound and forbidden certain freedoms.

Let me explain the intention of this analogy. The bound criminal deserves the restriction of freedom. Despite the fact that Christians deserve retribution, we have the chance to live free because of the blood of Jesus Christ. Unfortunately, many of God's children are living a bound and chained lifestyle, controlled and restricted by the enemy. Realize today that you, as a follower of Christ, are not entitled to the chained lifestyle controlled by bitterness, pride, unforgiveness, guilt, anger, lust, greed, insecurities, and sin.

Why does this bound condition seem so comparable to many Christians today? Why is the restriction of freedom happening so commonly among those who claim the name of Jesus Christ? The enemy knows what a threat we can be if we fully submit to God; therefore, he seeks to see living people walk in a dead condition. God desires to free you from the bondage and chains of this world. Once you accept Christ as your personal Savior, you no longer exist as property to this world but have become a child of the King.

It is an unfortunate reality that many of us who are Christians daily walk in a bound condition that does little to represent a life of salvation and freedom. We allow our voices to be silenced when God has something to say through us. We allow our hands to be tied when God desires to perform miracles through us. We allow our feet to be shackled when God desires to see us dance and rejoice in Him. We allow our ears to be blocked when He desires to speak directly to us.

GRAVE CLOTHES ARE OBJECTS OF A DEAD STATE OF BEING THAT RESTRICT THE FREEDOM OF A LIVING STATE OF BEING.

My heart identifies with John 11:43-44 in regard to what God wants to accomplish in each of our lives:

> Now when He had said these things, He cried with a loud voice, 'Lazarus, come forth!' [44]And he who had died came out bound hand and foot with grave clothes, and his face was wrapped with a cloth. Jesus said to them, 'Loose him, and let him go.'

Lazarus had been dead for a total of four days! God's glory was about to shine brightly as Jesus spoke the words, "Lazarus, come forth" to this deceased and decaying body. God's Word makes it obvious that Lazarus instantly came forth, but what happened next is very interesting.

Keep in mind that at that moment, Lazarus was alive and well! Jesus had spoken the word and God's power had given the dead body life once again. Read closely the description: upon awakening from the dead, Lazarus was still bound head to toe with grave clothes. **Ask the Lord to speak directly to your heart as you continue to read**. What happens next is extremely significant to the life of this formerly dead body and is equally relevant for you. The words spoken by Jesus to Lazarus in verse 44 are for each and every Christian on the face of the earth who feel bound and restricted by the dead condition that is no longer a part of your life. Carry the guilt and resentment no further. Lay sin and pride down. Open your heart, your mind, and your eyes to the reality that Jesus loves you! "LOOSE HIM, AND LET HIM GO!"

Be set free, dear Christian, from the bondage and chains associated with a person who has never experienced life in Jesus Christ. If you have received the gift of eternal salvation from God, then you are called forth and ordained as a living child to the King. Why would you desire to walk in the fashion of a dead man when your heart beats with life everlasting?

Lazarus lay dead for a total of four days. Once the power and love of Jesus pronounced him alive, how silly would it have looked for him to continue on with his life wrapped in the grave clothes? In the grave clothes, his hands and feet were bound, fully restricting him from working, serving, or walking. In grave clothes, his eyes and ears were muffled, hindering him from seeing clearly and communicating. In grave clothes, he looked like a dead person, fully hindering him from being an example of what it looked like to be alive!

The Holy Spirit will certainly uniquely apply this word to each individual, but for the purpose of application let's set a general definition for what we mean by "grave clothes." Grave clothes are objects of a dead state of being that restrict the freedom of a living state of being. Are there parts of your life prior to receiving Christ that keep you bound and chained? Be transparent and honest as you cry out before the Lord. He desires to loose you from those grave clothes! Are you a Christian who struggles with certain addictions or possesses a spirit of apathy or fear in the Christian walk? That is certainly a bound condition that restricts your hands and feet and your eyes and ears from being fully used by the Lord. God wants to free you from those grave clothes and send you forth exemplifying LIFE.

This is the heartbreaking condition today of far too many who have been given new life by our Lord Jesus Christ. There was that certain moment when He called your name: "(your name_____), come forth!" Jesus gave you life. How meaningless it would be for you to become a victim of the enemy's plot to deceive you and cause you to remain in a dead manner when absolute power and life are flowing through your veins.

God not only called us forth from a sinfully dead condition, but He urges us to loosen ourselves from the grave clothes that hinder our lives from being fully submitted to Him.

Does your past hinder you? Does pride dominate you? Does guilt break you? Does fear control you? Does bitterness defeat you? Grave clothes are not hard to identify if you honestly search your heart. They are the areas in your life that restrict your fellowship and freedom with Christ.

Be aware daily of the fact that the enemy desires to wrap and bind you so tightly that you can never live a life which reflects a living condition. He wants Christians around the globe to be so firmly bound that they never get to step forth in the authority and power God has planned for them. Sometimes it is because of a hurt they will not let God heal. Sometimes it is because of a specific sin that controls their lives. Regardless, they hinder the work of Christ when they refuse to once and for all rid their lives of the grave clothes.

The sole purpose of this introduction is to encourage and ignite the members of the Body of Christ to submit in obedience to the voice of the Lord and forever lay aside the grave clothes that seek to hinder their walks as vessels of God.

Nothing about the life of Lazarus testified to the resurrection power of Jesus Christ until he was freed from the conditions of the grave. What about you? Are you free from the conditions and identities of a dead person? If you have been redeemed as a child of God, the grave clothes are no longer for you. May you relinquish the grave clothes and live out your life as an ordained, anointed, living child of the Lord! Rely only on God's strength as you seek to move into a more intimate place with your Savior. He did it for Lazarus; He will do it for you.

"Bring me joy, bring me peace
Bring the chance to be free
Bring me anything that
brings You glory
And I know there'll be days
When this life brings me pain
But if that's what it takes
to praise you
Jesus, bring the rain."

—Mercy Me, *"Bring the Rain"*

CHAPTER ONE
Bring the Rain

As a child of Almighty God, it should be our desire to experience His presence the way Moses did on Mount Sinai. Though times have changed, one thing remains the same: God speaks and desires to be present in every aspect of our lives.

God began to speak to me personally through the song lyrics of "Bring the Rain" leading me to an experience with Him that transformed the course of my entire life. Discussing the details of that season in my life and my wife's life is challenging. It is, however, critical in connecting the reader to this writer and revealing how that experience exposed me to the voice of the Lord.

The birth of our son was the proudest moment of my entire

life. It took my relationship with Christ to a whole new level. I distinctly remember the evening he came into this world. My wife wanted to enjoy some chocolate ice-cream following the delivery. Eagerly, I headed to the nearest grocery store in search of exactly what she desired.

That night, I strolled through that store as if I had just hit the game winning homerun of the World Series! My heart longed for someone to see my hospital wrist band so that I might announce the great news. For the first time in my walk with the Lord, I understood what a sacrifice it was for the Father to give His only Son! For the first time in my life, I experienced the depth of His love for His children.

A little over a year passed, and being parents was such a blessing and certainly had a unique way of shaping our lives in a positive direction. My wife and I instantly understood what genuine selfless love was all about. We learned much and grew closer to the Lord as a result of this experience. However, God was not exactly done with the refining and molding of our lives. The upcoming season would prove to be one that brought my wife and me to our knees that we might gain a better view of what it meant to experience life solely for the purpose of glorifying the Lord.

Briefly review the words to the song that introduced this chapter:

"Bring me joy, bring me peace, bring the chance to be free, bring me anything that brings you glory. And I know there'll be days when this life brings me pain, but if that's what it takes to praise you, Jesus bring the rain."

In summary, the song says a servant's heart should desire ANYTHING that would allow God to be glorified. Whether it is joy, peace, pain, or heartache, would we be willing to accept it if it meant God being glorified and His Kingdom extended?

A year zipped by and my wife informed me that "number two" was "in progress." Sure I was excited, but feelings of nervousness and fear gripped me. We told family and friends the news and began to discuss this new chapter about to unfold in our lives. Devastating news, however, soon followed. Somewhere at the eight-week mark, we lost our baby.

I know this is a common occurrence among women, but until you have walked through it, you never fully grasp the pain. My wife and I prayed and cried together. It was difficult watching the love of my life ache with such sorrow. Once you find out you are expecting, you fall in love with that life. In that moment, God began to reveal to me how much His heart truly aches for us. "The peace of God which surpasses all understanding" (Philippians 4:7) flowed from Heaven to me. Having never even seen our baby, we loved him/her unconditionally. That manner of love was expressed on a much larger scale with Christ in that "before He formed us in the womb, He knew us" (Jeremiah 1:5). We are so precious to our Father.

Months passed by and then came those famous words, "I am pregnant" once again. My feelings were almost that of pure fear. I prayed against those feelings as I knew that they were not from the Lord. God told me in His Word that He does not give the spirit of fear, but rather the spirit of power and love and a sound mind (2 Timothy 1:7). The fear plaguing my life was a direct tool of the enemy.

The one thing I remember the most about that pregnancy was the hospital visits. Once you have experienced a sonogram that reveals heartbreaking news, as our previous experience had, it makes all future ones very intense. Fear literally conquered my body as we entered the exam room.

The room was dark. With trembling knees, I grasped my wife's hand and cried out to God for the life in her womb. I remember the look on our doctor's face and the tears that hit the floor as she told us that she detected no heartbeat.

The following weeks were rough. It was difficult to deal with telling everyone the news that the baby was no longer alive. All details aside, the evening came when our ten-week-old fetus was to naturally remove itself from my wife's body. We wanted to see if it would pass naturally and maybe avoid the DNC. That day came, and it would prove to be the single most life changing event of our entire lives. Tears fall even now as I pen these words.

As is the process of delivering a full term child, so it is with delivering an unborn ten-week-old. Together in our cabin, we prayed through it. Now please understand that I fully believe that those babies are real souls who now await us in Heaven. I looked to see if I could recognize anything that resembled a body so that I could pick him/her up. The thought of merely flushing my baby down the toilet was not acceptable. That may sound crazy to you, and it probably would be to me had I not walked right through it.

Many say a fetus that young is not recognizable. The first baby we lost was not as developed since he/she was not as far along. The second baby, however, opened my eyes fully to the glory of God!

I picked up something small, placed it in the palm of my hand, and held it very close to my eyes. My wife had left the bathroom with tears on her face, but I examined the fetus closely and saw the details of our baby's features. He or she was about the size of a large lima bean. I saw the eyes, the arms, the hands, the legs, and the feet. My wife overheard me and re-entered the room.

We were completely broken before the Lord. And, in that moment, the words to that song

> OUR HEARTS ALIGN WITH GOD'S HEART CREATING AN ATTITUDE OF SURRENDER.

flowed through my mind. God asked me, "Will you live to bring me glory?" Suddenly, I understood that I was not on this earth to glorify myself. I was here solely to glorify Him! Isaiah 42:8 says, "I am the LORD, that is My name; And My glory I will not give to another, Nor My praise to carved images." God said to me in a small, still voice, "This is not about you; you are here to honor and glorify Me."

Those words changed our lives! That event established a permanent passion within our hearts to be servants willing to do or go through anything that would allow Christ to be glorified. Stepping into that realm of submission allowed

God to receive praise and accomplish His purpose.

When we align our hearts and minds with that reality, we become serious threats to the enemy. Likewise, we place ourselves in a spiritual condition primed and ready for personal revival. In other words, our hearts align with God's heart creating an

> IS YOUR RELATIONSHIP WITH THE SAVIOR CHARACTERIZED BY A LIFE OF SUBMISSION?

attitude of surrender. In doing that, we show God with our lives that whether through joy, peace, pain, or trouble, we live to do His will. That spiritual condition equips us to be invincible to the plots of the enemy and creates what I consider a contagious faith that will spark national **revival**.

Prior to those events, I took a keen interest in the story of the blind man in John 9. Jesus and His disciples came across a man who was "blind from birth." The disciples asked Jesus a very interesting question in verse two: "Rabbi, who sinned, this man or his parents that he was born blind?"

Why did they automatically assume that the man's suffering was due to sin? Whatever the reason for their misunderstanding, they were about to have a new revelation. Jesus taught them a lesson concerning His glory. His response in verse three was, "Neither this man nor his parents sinned, but that the works of God should be made manifest or revealed in him."

If you finish the story, you will see how a young man stood alone for God's glory. Jesus had restored his sight, yet **nobody** was willing to accept that truth. They questioned him repeatedly, only to get the same response—that it was indeed Christ the Lord. His parents chickened out and would not defend him. Eventually, he was removed from the synagogue, but he remained steadfast with Christ!

That scripture brought me great comfort. I had constantly wondered if I had done something wrong to provoke such pain. Certainly sin does have consequences that may include suffering. However, God may use suffering as an avenue through which to bring Himself glory. All we have the ability to see is the here and now. God sees all. We are better off to trust Him.

This is not a pass to ignore sin. We all must examine our lives in order to pursue holy living; but understand that God may be refining you specifically for His glory. It hurts, but it will be worth it.

It is urgent that God's people hear His call! Arise and get ready. Prepare your heart to be moved and used in the fields that are white and ready to harvest. Beg the Lord to position your heart in a way that will prepare it to follow Him no matter the cost. Is your relationship with the Savior characterized by a life of submission? If the answer is "no," you are missing what He has for you. But take hope. If you honestly desire to reach that place, He **will** guide you there.

My prayer is that as you continue to read, the Holy Spirit of God will move and speak directly to your heart. You may be reading this on a couch, in a classroom, or in a bookstore. Wherever you are, fall to your knees and beg God to speak directly to your heart. My words may challenge you, but only God's Words will change you.

CHAPTER TWO
What do you have to say?

Aftere a few days of prayer and consideration, I feel led to continue our thoughts in the lesson from John chapter nine. The testimony from chapter one may seem a bit arbitrary in reference to the direction of this book, but it represents the moment when God began to reveal the urgency of the times for me and the present generation.

So often in life, it is convenient to turn our eyes from potential problems or confrontation. Parents, you know exactly what I am talking about! Imagine you are in a large gathering type of atmosphere and your little one is doing something that you know you would not tolerate at home. No one else notices, but you do. The easiest thing for you to do is let it go.

On a much larger scale, this is happening among God's

people in today's society. Fear of "rocking the boat" muzzles the cry for righteousness from the lips of Christians. Let me be the first to confess that I am as guilty as the next person.

Slowly, the enemy is creating compromise and brain washing the minds of those who claim to be followers of Christ. Slowly, the children of the Lord are drifting off to sleep. There we are, lying on the couch allowing the enemy to fill the minds of God's people with deception and lies while God says, "WAKE UP!" (Isaiah 52:1)

That truth hit me during the early morning hours in December 2009. In the cozy atmosphere of my life's comfort zone, my urgency and passion for the Lord had experienced compromise. Essentially, that created spiritual lethargy. It had always been a practical truth to my everyday life, but all of a sudden something clicked.

That morning, my almost three-year-old son had awakened an hour or so before he normally did. He refused to lie back down at that moment, so I thought I would take him to our living room where we could fall back to sleep on the sofa. Nice try!

My next move was one that I thought was sure to generate a few moments of rest for me. Yes, that's right, I turned on some cartoons. Now considering we only got a few channels at our house, I figured that one cartoon would be just fine. I turned it on and lay beside my son preparing to drift back to sleep. What happened next was one of those moments when you feel as if you directly heard the voice of God.

My son's ears and eyes were fixed intently upon the sounds

and characters in the show, and just as I was about to close my eyes for those few precious moments of rest, I saw it. On the screen, I observed symbols that represented beliefs in cults and false doctrines. The characters were talking about or mimicking the act of casting spells. Suddenly, as clearly as I had ever heard a command, God said, "Wake up! Wake up! While you rest there, the enemy is on the prowl. Wake up, son!"

> FEAR OF "ROCKING THE BOAT" MUZZLES THE CRY FOR RIGHTEOUSNESS FROM THE LIPS OF CHRISTIANS.

How does that incident relate to John chapter nine? As we continue to read the story, we find the healing of that blind man caused quite a stir in a community dominated by legalism and erroneous religious thought. Let's take a look together, **but first pray and ask the Holy Spirit to speak directly to your heart! Ask Him to change your heart forever**.

In verses 8-10, we clearly see the confusion among the people concerning the identity of the formerly blind man. They were shocked and filled with uncertainty, unsure if he was even the same person who had once fumbled through the streets. The problem could not be resolved by the people, so they carried the man before the Pharisees. They interrogated him multiple times because they were unwilling to accept Jesus as the Healer.

Look at verse 16 for a moment. Jesus performed that miracle on the Sabbath. In light of that, the Pharisees considered

Him a law-breaking sinner. Sadly, they were so trapped by incorrect mindsets they could not experience His love!

Verse 17 presents a powerful question that served as the true test to the blind man:

> They said to the blind man again, "What do you say about Him because He opened your eyes?" He said, "He is a prophet."
>
> —John 9:17

Read the question over and over again, understanding that He has done the same for us. That was the moment of truth. The blind man could have said a multitude of other things and compromised his faith. He could have taken the easy way out and turned his head at that uncomfortable situation! In short, he could have been like his parents in verses 21 and 22. When asked if it was indeed Jesus who had opened the eyes of their son, they had responded this way:

> "But by what means he now sees we do not know, or who opened his eyes we do not know. He is of age; ask him. He will speak for himself." His parents said these things because they feared the Jews, for the Jews had agreed already that if anyone confessed that He was Christ, he would be put out of the synagogue.
>
> —John 9:21-22

Listen closely because what you just read is the "bury your head in the sand" mentality that plagues the church today.

Imagine what went through the mind of that man. Not even his parents were willing to stand in the gap for fear of the rejection and persecution of man. If you think that broke their son's heart, can you imagine how it felt to our Father? Why did they do it? It was easier to keep quiet than to rock the boat. Verse 22 tells us they feared being put out of the synagogue.

Only one person was kicked out of the synagogue that day; but despite the fact that the entire community and his parents were against him, the young man stood firm in the name of Christ. Compromise would have been so easy in that moment. But there was one huge problem. He had experienced a real and powerful God who he knew would never leave his side.

He may have stood alone before the Pharisees, but look who was first to meet him after he was removed from the synagogue. Verse 35 reveals how much God honors a servant who will be bold for His truth!

> Jesus heard that they had cast him out; and when He
> had found him, He said to him, "Do you believe in
> the Son of God?"
>
> —John 9:35

Jesus gave him sight physically—now it was about to happen spiritually! What an ending to a story of courage and boldness for the Lord, as the man in verse 38 proclaims, "Lord, I believe!"

If you are like me, the whole stance of the formerly blind

man's parents is troubling; but what about us? How many times have we done the same thing and broken the heart of our Savior?

God is not asking us to be rude or mean. He is asking us to stand up for the name of Christ. Where? In our homes, our schools, our churches, our government.

> REVIVAL BEGINS IN A
> HEART SUBMITTED ONLY
> TO THE VOICE OF GOD.

The voice of the Lord and the voice of God's children cannot be heard if it continues to be muzzled by man. The silence created by this muzzle puts us in jeopardy of spiritual apathy/sleep. Let me assure you that sleep is something the enemy never does. He constantly seeks to deceive us and destroy our lives.

The easy thing to do is "keep quiet" or "stay out of it." However, when you have an encounter with Christ that alters your life, it is impossible to sit on the sidelines and watch the truth compromised. What do you have to say, God's people? What do **you** have to say about the One who opened your blind eyes?

Revival begins in a heart submitted only to the voice of God. In that condition, our burning desire is to reveal the Gospel message in a fashion that contagiously infects all those we contact. Think of how simple it is compared to how difficult we seek to make it. God opened our blind eyes and gave us life. If it was a real encounter, there is no way you and I would allow friends, family, government, religion, or any other factor to prohibit us from announcing His grace and love from the mountain tops.

I will end this chapter with this final note. Right before His death, Jesus was in the Garden of Gethsemane in deep prayer. In Matthew chapter 26, He urged His disciples to sit and watch while He prayed before the Father. He returned to find them fast asleep. His response:

> Then He came to the disciples and found them sleeping, and said to Peter, "What! Could you not watch with Me one hour? [41] Watch and pray, lest you enter into temptation. The spirit indeed is willing, but the flesh is weak."
>
> —Matthew 26:40-41

That scripture characterizes the bulk of Christianity today—but that will change. However, let us focus personally. Are you in a condition of sleep? Do you hear God's voice urging you to arise? Stand to your feet and tell God that from now on you will be bold for His name! Refuse to allow anything associated with this world to hinder who He has ordained you to be. If He is your Savior, then you are His spokesperson. You are cherished, loved, and ordained from Heaven to impact this world in the name of Jesus.

CHAPTER THREE
Change Your Lenses

Viewing my life from the perspective that I was fashioned strictly to glorify the Father created a paradigm shift in my life. For years in my Christian walk, I saw my life through the lens of man. That essentially created a selfish and prideful nature that surely broke the heart of the One who gave me life.

The very moment I began to view my life—past, present, and future—from a Heavenly perspective, a significant level of freedom was unveiled. The freedom that I should have enjoyed in Christ had become restricted because I had not allowed my life to become solely focused on honoring my Father above all else.

If you want freedom from hurt, pain, bitterness, guilt, worry, burdens, and other trials associated with this fallen world, change your lens. Let go of the earthly perspective that hinders fellowship with the Lord. Receive a Heavenly perspective that allows you to view the circumstances of your life through the eyes of Christ.

God has a **specific** will and plan for each and every person He creates, and only through submission to His voice can it be found. He paid the ultimate price to redeem His children, and all those who receive that precious gift can rest assured that He will always lead and guide them. With that being said, God also knows exactly what He must take us through in order to get our hearts and lives in position to further His Kingdom.

As a child of God, do you desire to be a vessel through which He can flow to accomplish His purpose and plan? In no way, shape, or form is that some sort of sentence to a life of misery. On the contrary, accepting a Heavenly perspective grants you liberty and happiness that cannot be hindered by the enemy or your circumstances.

I hope you understand my heart when I say this, but a follower of Christ like you who receives the Heavenly call to live only for the purpose of glorifying God will be INVINCIBLE. In other words, the same situations that once defeated you will no longer prevail. Why? Despite not knowing what He is doing through your circumstance, your Heavenly perspective will remind you that He knows the "bigger picture." You will rejoice in sorrow. You will praise Him through the pain.

And all the while, your beautiful God will receive the glory and honor that only He deserves.

Here is the question for consideration. Are you willing to allow the sovereign hand of God to align and position your life such that only He can be glorified? What if it means losing a job? What if it means losing the life of a loved one? What if it means pain and hurt?

Please do not read this and assume I am suggesting that God is out to make your life miserable and you despondent. This is an absolute lie. Matthew 7:11 indicates that God desires to provide for you and love you far beyond the expressions of love you are capable of rendering.

Understand that I do not doubt the unconditional love of Christ. What I am trying to illustrate is that God, in His perfect sovereignty, knows exactly where you need to be. If you want to walk a life completely surrendered to making the name of Jesus known around the world, get ready for the refining process.

> GOD ALSO KNOWS EXACTLY WHAT HE MUST TAKE US THROUGH IN ORDER TO GET OUR HEARTS AND LIVES IN POSITION TO FURTHER HIS KINGDOM.

Consider the testimony I spoke of in the opening of this book. If someone had asked my wife and me prior to the circumstance occurring if we wanted to face that season, we would have immediately responded, "No!" Speaking presently, we know we could never have progressed in our relationship and walk with the Lord without it. That process was His positioning. He had to do something to get us where He wanted us to be.

Let us consider the life of Esther. We certainly have a general understanding of how God used her life to bring deliverance to His people. But let me ask you this: How did Esther get in that position? Do you think she happened to live nearby and receive an offer from the king? Absolutely not! Esther's life presents an amazing journey of refining, suffering, and positioning in order for her to perform and walk in the purpose for which Christ had created her.

First of all, consider why Esther was raised and instructed by her cousin, Mordecai. Esther 2:6-7 reveals that she had been carried away into Babylonian exile and that she had lost her father and mother to death:

> Kish had been carried away from Jerusalem with the captives who had been captured with Jeconiah king of Judah, whom Nebuchadnezzar the king of Babylon had carried away. 7And Mordecai had brought up Hadassah, that is, Esther, his uncle's daughter, for she had neither father nor mother. The young woman was lovely and beautiful. When her father and mother died, Mordecai took her as his own daughter.

If you are like me, we read this and jump on over to the next verse to continue the story. But hold for a few moments. To lose a mother or father, especially during your formidable years, is devastating. What kind of emotions do you think Esther, then Hadassah, experienced? Pain, sorrow, and grief had surely gripped her life as she lost her mother and father and was essentially carried away into exile. Do you think Hadassah knew the meaning of this tragedy? Perhaps thoughts of discouragement and doubt dominated her life. Maybe she felt as if God had abandoned her. Keep in mind, brothers and sisters in the Lord, Hadassah was being positioned.

Hallelujah—God knows the bigger picture. Let us back up and witness another powerful move of God. In chapter one verses 10-12, we read about Queen Vashti and her refusal to obey the king's command. Stop right there. Why would a lady in the highest royal position put her future in jeopardy? Because God needed to get his royal servant in position, therefore, the current holder of that position needed to be removed.

Then comes the favor God's children receive as they walk steadfastly after His voice. In Esther 2:17, we read, "the king loved Esther more than all the women, and she found favor and kindness with him more than all the virgins." Why do you think such favor rested with Esther? Was it so she could assume the royal position to merely serve King Ahasuerus? Absolutely not! She was being positioned by the King of the universe for "such a time as this"!

How do you think Esther felt as she journeyed along the path to where God was leading? She was removed from her home and stripped of her mother and father, perhaps three of the greatest comforts known to man. She was raised by an older cousin under a hidden identity. She was made to endure a yearlong purification process just to be a mere option for the King Ahasuerus.

I wonder whether or not Esther asked the same question I often tend to ask: "God what are you up to?" I wonder if she ever felt alone, sad, or discouraged. I wonder if she ever felt as if God had forgotten about her.

> TOO MANY MEMBERS OF THE ARMY OF GOD ARE FALLING ASIDE BECAUSE THEY ARE DECEIVED BY THE PHILOSOPHIES OF MAN.

The reality is: God had a unique and divine plan for Hadassah's life. That reality surely dawned on her when Mordecai said:

> "For if you remain completely silent at this time, relief and deliverance will arise for the Jews from another place, but you and your father's house will perish. Yet who knows whether you have come to the kingdom for such a time as this?"
>
> —Esther 4:14

Open your Bible and read that verse six or seven times. Haman plotted his evil scheme and endangered the life of every Jew. The discussion between Esther and Mordecai in chapter four is incredible as it reveals a shift in Esther's perspective from earthly to Heavenly. Esther knows that because of custom it will cost her life to approach the King and plead for her people. With the help of Mordecai, it dawns on her—she was created for that moment!

Have you considered that this may indeed be how God moves within your life and mine? One major problem: We as Christians are missing our personal "such a time as this" because we are brainwashed by man's ideology that says if we do not prosper, then something must be wrong with our lives.

Certainly some suffering is a result of sin and some a result of the fallen world in which we currently live, but has it ever dawned on you that God could be leading you through a storm simply to better equip you personally for a specific purpose He had in mind when he formed you? Too many times we go through the suffering only to abandon God and be left wondering what happened. When we do that, we fully deny the divine positioning of the hand of God.

Let us look to Esther 4:14 for an explanation. What does Mordecai say? "If you hold your peace, God will get the job done and the Jews will be delivered. But what if you were created specifically for this moment, and you walk away?" Esther's life had been an incredible journey. Now, she had a decision to make. Was she going to trust the divine leading of Almighty God and allow her life and her circumstances to glorify His name and complete His work?

She certainly could have remained silent, but she would have missed the entire purpose of her positioning. Esther could have given up in the midst of the battle. However, because of her ability to view her circumstances through the Heavenly lens, she knew this journey was not about Esther; it was about God. The heavenly perspective says, "If I perish, I perish" (Esther 4:16), because I desire to live to glorify the Father.

I do realize this is intense and that many will not read another word of this book. Too many members of the army of God are falling aside because they are deceived by the philosophies of man. That is not to say or imply in any way that Christians must live unhappy, sorrowful lives. That is clearly not the case.

Let's be completely honest—regardless of our stance on suffering versus prosperity—we can all agree that hard times do arise. No person can run from or deny the fact that this current world lends its share of pain. Will Christians become a product of that pain and be controlled by it? Or will they shift their thinking by the power of the Holy Spirit to view progress through this life from a Heavenly perspective?

Stop right now; pray and ask the Holy Spirit to help you recall your journey to this point in life.

1. Are there hurts and pains that seem confusing and leave you with questions?

2. Can you identify how God may have used them to shape or position you for His purpose?

3. What steps can you take to change the way you view circumstances that once defeated you?

He will show you the areas where you were "corrected" due to sin. But ask Him to take you further. Some may see broken homes, abuse, neglect, poverty, and other things. I encourage you in the name of Jesus Christ; do not let those be your excuse or crutch. Do not let them lead to hurt, resentment, and bitterness that hinder who God originally designed you to be. Ask Him to transform your thinking from earthly to Heavenly.

As you begin to experience this shift, it will no longer become about you. Rather, you can rejoice knowing the divine Creator of this world has the perfect plan. At the very moment of conception, God knew what he wanted to do with you. The enemy certainly would love nothing more than to rob and steal your destiny from you. You do not have to let him.

Deny and rebuke any thoughts of feeling sorry for yourself. God has a special, unique, and powerful plan for your life. Christian, He has been shaping you all the way. He plans to position you for His glory.

"How does this make me invincible?" you might ask. Consider this analogy with an honest heart. Say you hear of a mother and father who lost a teenager in a car accident. You hurt for them and express sorrow, but do you mourn and wail as if the child were your own? No. Why? It was not really about you.

Teenager, you hear about a sixteen-year-old boy who loses his brother in war. You grieve and express sorrow for him, but do you experience the kind of hurt that that sixteen-year-old brother is facing? No. Why? It is not really about you.

If you are honest, you will admit to experiencing those things personally. The same can be said for changing our lenses from earthly to Heavenly. When we Christians can understand and acknowledge that this life is not about us but is about the name and glory of Jesus Christ, it will take away much of the pain associated with tough times. Why? It is not really about us.

Please understand my heart. Behind this pen is not some man who yearns to experience hurt. None of us wants that. And I am not suggesting that your life will fall apart and that death is at your family's doorstep if you follow God's words. My heart desires to no longer see God's children robbed and distracted by difficult circumstances.

If you are presently in a difficult circumstance, don't lie down and quit. Persevere in prayer at all times. God may indeed be positioning you. This is never an excuse to give up. Fight and pray until you have clarity. I will confess to you that I prayed life into the child in my wife's womb until the day the baby was released, regardless of what hospital machines told me.

What I do not want Christians to do with the information in this chapter is to give up saying, "Well, this must be God's will." Sure, we all want God's will, but fight and pray and cling to the garment of Jesus until the storm is over. With the Heavenly perspective, we place our emotion and will in His hands. That allows Him to position us so that our lives may bring glory to His name.

I pray continuously when I have a burdened heart for a specific request. One particular day, a person somewhat rebuked me for the continual prayer saying, "God may want them to struggle with that forever." While I acknowledge that could be a true statement, I do not believe God wants us to write off the authority and power we Christians have in communicating with Him.

I asked this person to look at Matthew 26:39. If anyone has ever walked the face of this earth and specifically known His purpose, it was Jesus Christ. Yet, in verse 39, He says, "If it be possible, let this cup pass from me." Although He immediately followed with a statement yielding to the will of His Father, Jesus yearned for deliverance.

I realize this seems a bit off track, but I knew this chapter might provoke a critic to assume I approve of lazy Christianity. We need to fight for life. We need to war against the power of the enemy, knowing that we operate under the authority of the living God. You must refuse to allow trials—whether past, present or future—to discourage or defeat you. God wants to position you specifically so you can reign for Him.

Let me encourage you with a testimony about "not holding your peace" and about being God's instrument anywhere and everywhere. My family and I were vacationing at the beach one summer when God did an incredible thing. My oldest son and I stopped in a local grocery store to get a few items. He sat on my shoulders as we approached the frozen food section and the dairy/meat department. Directly in front of me stood a man with his young son picking out some sort of cold grocery product.

I stopped and looked at them because I felt a significant urge from God to speak to him. I guess I stared long enough because he finally looked into my eyes. The lengthy eye contact must have been awkward and scary for this man.

Well, what do you think I did? That's right; I hauled freight and fled the scene! Hold on, this gets better. The entire time my son and I shopped, conviction over missing an assignment consumed me. We checked out, and when we got to our car, there they were! I watched the man and his son get into their truck as we pulled out of the parking lot. I even ended up behind them at the stop light.

My mind was reeling at that point and praying for God to show me what to do next. I followed the man down the road and actually considered following him to his house. (Surely that would have scared him to death!)

As I always do when I feel as if I missed an assignment, I prayed for the man from the car, hoping that would be satisfactory to the Lord. Yeah right! As soon as I returned to our rental house, I told my wife about the encounter and how terribly guilty I felt about not speaking. I had held my peace, and it had not set too well with me.

We finished our vacation week, and on the final evening, we drove out on the empty beaches to take pictures together before leaving for home. I am not exaggerating when I say that as far as the eye could see, there was nobody else out that evening. And yet, I noticed a truck following close behind us, and it was obvious the people in it were out cruising. Frustrated at the invasion of privacy, I pulled over. Sure enough, they stopped about 30 feet away. Come on, I thought. This whole beach is vacant and they want to follow us!

We decided to stick with our spot and got out of the vehicle. I looked over and almost lost my breath. It was the same truck from the grocery store. I looked closer and out jumped a man with his wife and son. That place was a huge vacation destination, and the odds of even seeing the same person twice was rare, yet there I was, side by side with my assignment once again.

> THERE WILL COME THAT MOMENT IN YOUR LIFE WHEN YOU WILL STAND FACE TO FACE WITH YOUR DESTINY.

Believe it or not, I was still struggling about whether or not to approach the man. Can you believe that! God wanted to speak to the man and He wanted to use me. As I wrestled with my fear, I looked around and noticed the man's wife approaching our vehicle. She offered to take a picture of our family together.

Enough was enough! I walked straight over to the man and revealed what the Lord wanted me to say. And do you know what happened? NOTHING! He looked at me like I was somewhat crazy; then we shook hands and bid farewell to one another.

I may never know what the purpose of that encounter was,

but regardless, God wanted my submissive obedience. If I had held my peace on that final encounter on the beach that evening, I may have missed a divine calling from the Heavens. Just because lightning bolts didn't flash when I spoke to the man is irrelevant. The only relevant factor when God speaks to us is our full submission to His command. Although I may never know, my heart tells me that our meeting on the beach was a game changer not only for that man but for me as well.

There will come that moment in your life when you will stand face to face with your destiny. You have a huge decision to make in that instant. Will you respond to the voice of the Lord, or will you allow your circumstances to distract you from the purpose for which you were created?

Esther endured serious pain that she might be positioned by the hand of God. The favor of the Lord resided with her in those situations, not because she deserved it, but because through that favor, God would be glorified.

Have you ever considered the favor of God in your life from this angle? His favor in our lives is certainly not because you or I have earned it. It is strictly to bring God glory; and if we view it in any other fashion, we are missing the point. When life's journey becomes about us, our God, also known as Jealous (Exodus 34:14), is being robbed of His glory. It is not about you. It is not about me. It is about Him!

CHAPTER FOUR
Abiding or Abusing

The single greatest hindrance to my walk and fellow-ship with Jesus Christ has been extreme fear. God's Word is clear that a spirit of fear is not of Him. Fear of failure, fear of the night, fear of sickness—all have been considerable at various stages throughout my life. Of the ones previously mentioned, however, fear of the night and the presence of evil have significantly troubled me at various times.

I remember when I was a child watching out my bedroom window while everyone else slept to make sure my home was being monitored. I actually lost so much sleep that my grades in school began to suffer. For a short season, at the age of twelve, I relied on sleeping pills just to enable me to gain a restful night.

Those struggles followed me through school and into my marriage. Now when you are a ten-year-old boy scared of the dark, it is a little understandable. When you are in your early twenties, it becomes embarrassing. At various stages of my life, fear literally suffocated me. I prayed often, rebuking any and all generational issues or demonic presences that might be causing me grief. As is the case with many Christians, Psalm 91 became an instrumental passage that brought great comfort to my life—especially at night.

God wants you to know that despite any suffering or trial that may accompany your life, as one of His disciples, He is and desires to be your comforting shadow.

Darkness has always been the big kicker for me. I will go anywhere, anytime alone—until it gets dark. One night, that issue took a significant shift. Peering out my window, praying as I did before night hours, I looked into the face of the darkness and simply asked God why it had such power over me. He revealed this to me, "If you will abide in me, this will not be darkness but the **SHADOW** of my wings!" Excitement instantaneously filled my soul. "But wait Lord," I said, "I am your child. Do I not abide in You already?" As we examine Psalm 91, ask God if you are truly abiding in Him.

What does it mean to abide? Abiding is the constant state of residing in or under something. To abide in Christ means security, comfort, and provision; you remain connected because without that connection there could be serious consequences.

Examine your heart, Christian. Do you truly abide under the shadow every moment of every day? The answer to that question during that difficult season of my life was "no." I was abusing the shadow not abiding in it. How did I abuse the shadow? The best way I can explain it is with a raincoat analogy. When it is raining, what do most people do with a raincoat? Put it on. What generally happens to the raincoat when the rain is over? It gets put away. Our Lord should not and will not be treated that way. That is called abusing the shadow of the Almighty, not abiding in it!

Verse one of Psalm 91 tells the Christian exactly how to abide under the shadow of the Almighty:

> He who dwells in the secret place of the Most
> High shall abide under the shadow of the Almighty.
> —Psalm 91:1

Once we grasp this scripture, we can toss every "how to" success formula directly into the trash. God gives us the answer: **Live in the secret place**. Live in a place of constant fellowship and intimacy with God. Live in a place where your heart begins to beat and strive for the things of God's heart. It is a day in and day out communion with the Son that you have no plans to break. The place in which you abide ultimately shapes who you are as an individual. It is true physically. It is true spiritually.

People go to the hospital to get well; then they desire to go home. Families go on vacation for recreation and relaxation, but they do not stay there because it is not their home. Jesus Christ does not want to be our temporary help, then be set aside 'till needed again. In fact, God is not fooled by that sort of behavior, nor will He tolerate it from his followers. Are you guilty of abusing the shadow? Run to the secret place and beg God to direct your steps as you seek to turn from that condition.

If you are like me, you often tend to view the actions of the children of Israel with harsh criticism. Time after time they were in situations where their only hope for strength and survival was God Almighty. And time and time again, He faithfully delivered them.

Deuteronomy 8:11-18 lends a strong warning to Christians today about the danger of abusing the shadow rather than faithfully abiding in it. God had delivered the children of Israel and had multiplied every single area of their lives— their flocks, their wealth, their homes, their families. The Lord had miraculously brought them from bondage to freedom. Look at verse 15:

> Who led you through that great and terrible wilderness, in which were fiery serpents and scorpions and thirsty land where there was no water; who brought water for you out of the flinty rock;
>
> —Deuteronomy 8:15

God sovereignly guided His children through the difficulties of the wilderness and guarded them against drought, serpents, and other hardships. Do you think they cried out to the Father for deliverance while journeying through these places? Sure they did.

In Judges 6:7, while held captive by the Midianites, the children of Israel "cried unto the Lord." And yes, God heard their cries and brought their deliverance. Why? In addition to the fact that He loved them, their hearts were finally in a condition of humility and full dependence upon Him.

That is the position that God desires our hearts to be in at all times—not just when we need Him here and there. The sovereign hand of God permitted their bondage in order that the Israelites would learn to fully depend upon Him. We never know how much we truly need Him until we have been completely stripped of our securities. That condition enables full dependence.

Going back to Deuteronomy 8, let us take a look at what abusing the shadow looks like:

> Beware that you do not forget the LORD your God by
> not keeping His commandments and His ordinances
> and His statutes which I am commanding you today.
> —Deuteronomy 8:11

Verse 11 begins with the word BEWARE. What do you immediately think of when you see that word written in large letters? Having had the misfortune of being frightened by many chases by dogs, "Beware of Dogs" is the first thing that pops into my mind. Beware always means watch out, stay away, or get ready for some sort of attack.

God is serious about the words written in this verse, and

although it was indeed written as a warning to His children as He led them towards the Promised Land, we can learn and apply much from it to our lives as well. "Do not forget the Lord your God." When times were tough, the Israelites had no one to lean on but God. However, now that times were good, they were committing the heartbreaking mistake of turning their hearts from intimacy with Him.

Look at what they say in verse 17: "my power and the might of mine hand hath begotten me this wealth." How could they do that to the Lord? How could they treat their loving, gracious, compassionate Lord with such disrespect?

Just when I begin to critique and ridicule the children of Israel for such atrocious acts towards God's love, the Lord says, "Wait a minute; take a close look at your heart." How many times had I cried out to God when in bondage, yet forgotten all about Him when things appeared to be going just fine. How many times had I abused that shadow?

Ask God here to reveal the depths of your heart. Allow Him to show you these areas of your life where you may have treated Him as if He were a mere raincoat.

I will try to explain my heart, but words seem inadequate. Over and over again I have treated the Lord and Savior as a raincoat rather than as the love of my life.

I have had to deal with death many times. In those moments, I remember praying what felt like every hour of every day. I have been at those crossroads relating to job/ministry where a decision needed to be made that would certainly alter my life. I have battled through emotional and spiritual issues so intense that had I not spent time with Him, I felt I would have surely died. Yet as a minister and student of the Bible, I have found myself in other seasons where the **only** occasion in which I spent time with the Lord was when I either needed to complete a college assignment or preach a sermon. In other words, I spent time with Him because I needed Him to help me prepare to enhance my performance and not because I hungered for the Word. At those times, I spent very little time at the feet of Jesus. Talk about abusing the shadow!

Can you honestly relate to any of these situations? I am certain that every single person reading this book has a similar testimony to share. Please do not misunderstand, God does want us to pray and cry out to Him. He loves our heart to be in the condition of full focus and reliance upon Him. And He wants it ALL THE TIME.

Does this next scenario sound familiar as well? The bills are paid; everyone is healthy; church is great; marriage is great; all is well—so let me kick back and enjoy. Is there something wrong with enjoying blessings? "No!" Here is my point. Compare the blessings of the previous sentence to difficult scenarios such as death, pain, and sorrow. Can you honestly say that your heart craved Jesus as much when all was fine as it did when it seemed as if the world crumbled all around you?

> I will say to the LORD, "My refuge and my fortress,
> My God, in whom I trust!"
> Surely He shall deliver you from the snare of the

fowler

And from the perilous pestilence.

He shall cover you with His feathers

And under His wings you shall take refuge;

His truth shall be your shield and buckler.

You shall not be afraid of the terror by night,

Nor for the arrow that flies by day;

Nor of the pestilence that walks in darkness,

Nor of the destruction that lays waste at noonday.

A thousand may fall at your side

And ten thousand at your right hand.

But it shall not come near you.

—Psalm 91:2-7

Not a person walking this earth would reject the promises offered in this chapter of Psalms. We want protection. We want peace. We want deliverance. Let's be sincere; we all need it every single day. But please hear the words clearly. If you and I simply desire to dwell in the secret place JUST to receive the benefits from the shadow, we are once again guilty of abusing the precious gift God offers.

This is not some kind of step-by-step formula granting you all the blessings that you desire. Please understand the heart of the Lord here. The only way a person can truly abide in the shadow of the Almighty is by DWELLING IN THE SECRET PLACE. To **live** under the shadow, you must **live** in the secret place. You cannot have one without the other.

Dwelling in the secret place is seeking intimacy with Him with every ounce of who you are. That is, your heart and soul and mind crave only to fall more and more in love with Jesus with each passing moment of the day. It is spending time with Him. It is praising Him. It is dancing before Him. It is serving Him—all the time—not just in the good or bad, but always. Psalm 91 is not something you can just pick up and use because it happens to be convenient. It is not a potion or formula. It is a benefit of clinging to the heart of Jesus.

We can fool a lot of people, but we cannot fool God. He knows whether or not we are truly interested in knowing Him more or if we just want the security described in Psalm 91. Our security and protection should never be the reason for desiring the shadow. We should desire the shadow because we are head over heels in love with Jesus and nothing satisfies our heart's longings the way He does. Why do you think the entire Psalm begins with that statement, "He that dwells in the secret place?" It is not a prescription; it is a condition of the heart.

> PSALM 91 IS NOT SOMETHING YOU CAN JUST PICK UP AND USE BECAUSE IT HAPPENS TO BE CONVENIENT. IT IS NOT A POTION OR FORMULA. IT IS A BENEFIT OF CLINGING TO THE HEART OF JESUS.

If God has revealed anything to your heart, ask Him what He wants you to do about it. Try not to beat yourself up if you feel as if you have failed in this area. Repent and know that

God is concerned about this moment forward. Remember Christian, you are a dear, sweet child of the King. He wants you to desire Him with passion that far surpasses any other passions within your life.

If He has revealed this to you—and you desire a life committed to abiding in that secret place where you don't care about anything but loving Him more—He will give it to you. God's Word in Psalm 91 reveals the promises of a life committed to intimacy with Him. What if none of these promises—hope, protection, peace, security—were promised, would you still want the secret place? The answer to that question will reveal the intentions of your heart.

Disobedience led God's children to many years of bondage and wandering. The same has been true for my life and perhaps for the lives of some of you reading this book. May the words "redemption" and "restoration" echo through your mind as you move beyond your past and toward your expectation for your future. His shadow is a powerful and refreshing place. The humble submissive act of dwelling in the secret place will take you there.

CHAPTER FIVE
The Man Under Authority

It is amazing what people can accomplish even outside the realm of a Christ-centered way of life. Self-made millionaires increase by the masses year after year in the Western world. While that certainly stands as an obvious blessing, mankind driven by the flesh has successfully transformed that blessing into the worst curse ever to strike America. Those successes have become the driving force behind the mentality of work, work, work, and prevail, prevail, prevail.

Before we continue, please get one thing clear in your heart and mind: This writer in no way, shape, or form condones laziness or any form of apathy. I have performed physical labor since I was twelve years of age and thoroughly enjoy and appreciate God's design for man to work. What we are about to discuss, as with every topic in this book, concerns the intentions of the heart, not the mere action of your flesh.

The same success that plagues the American visionary also plagues the Church. Having the best programs, the largest congregation, the finest facilities, the sweetest sermons, or the best workers have all somehow managed to take preeminence over the Holy Spirit of God. Why? We care more about the approval of man than the approval of God. How the Holy Spirit of God feels is second or even third in importance.

Please be transparent here and allow God to speak.

As a youth leader several years ago, I began having over a hundred youth on a given Wednesday night at a local church. That may sound tiny to those from big cities, but in a small country town, it was fabulous. Two years passed, a few went to college, and one night I found myself staring at fifteen hungry souls.

> WE CARE MORE ABOUT THE APPROVAL OF MAN THAN THE APPROVAL OF GOD.

Based on every church growth method and certainly the opinion of man, my ministry was a failure. But as I began to complain and wonder what in the world I had done wrong, God reminded me that He would send who He wanted to send and He would perform the work. He only needed me to be His vessel.

If you are like me, severe guilt causes you to accept more

tasks than you are humanly capable of handling. If I was not driving a bus route, I felt I was not showing God I loved Him. If I was not attending every church outreach that took place, then I did not truly love Jesus. So what did I do? I went to every meeting, and I drove the bus every time, despite the fact that I often deserted my own wife and children to do those things.

Let us be authentic here. The enemy used the classic and subtle tool of busyness to distract me from the most important aspect of my life—my relationship with Jesus Christ. For that reason, Luke 10:38-42 became pivotal in transforming my way of thinking:

> Now it happened as they went that He entered a certain village; and a certain woman named Martha welcomed Him into her house. [39]And she had a sister called Mary, who also sat at Jesus' feet and heard His word. [40]But Martha was distracted with much serving, and she approached Him and said, "Lord, do you not care that my sister has left me to serve alone? Therefore tell her to help me." [41] And Jesus answered and said to her, "Martha, Martha, you are worried and troubled about many things. [42]But one thing is needed, and Mary has chosen that good part, which will not be taken away from her."

The Scripture is clear here and needs little interpretation. I am certain the majority of you reading right now have already been introduced to this passage, but I want to highlight verse 42.

Prior to that verse, of course, we see the interaction between Martha, Mary (sisters of Lazarus), and Jesus. Martha had worked hard to prepare for Jesus, but verse 40 reveals that her abundant "serving" was a **distraction.** It was not that serving was wrong, but the serving had caused her to be distracted from the presence of Jesus.

Now let's place the focus on verse 42 for a moment. Here sat Mary at the feet of Jesus Christ. Listen to the words Jesus used to describe her actions: "Mary hath chosen that good part, which shall not be taken away from her." Compare that to His description of Martha: "thou art worried and troubled about many things."

When that passage came alive to me personally, it altered the course of my life. Give the question serious consideration. Do you honestly feel like your life/ministry (I put the two together because every part of the life of a believer should be a ministry of Jesus) is one characterized by loving the calling rather than the caller? Do the words "distracted," "worried," or "troubled" describe your relationship with Jesus? Or do you have the peace and joy that come only from abiding in the presence of the Savior?

The part of verse 42 that excites me most is the concept of our intimacy with Him being something that nothing on the face of this earth can touch. Think about the things that distract us from Jesus. How **secure** are they?

What about our jobs? Probably the most inconsistent ground we walk on is related to vocation. The average job probably consumes 50 to 60 times more of our time than our fellowship with the One who gives us the ability to perform that job. Many of you have experienced it first hand and all certainly know that a job can be taken away.

The list can go on and on—just fill in the blanks. We lose family members, we lose positions, we lose finances, we lose security, and we lose comfort. But remember, there is one thing that cannot be taken away,

> A GENUINE HEART OF SERVICE MUST ALWAYS AND ONLY FLOW OUT OF AN INTIMATE RELATIONSHIP WITH JESUS.

and that is our relationship with Jesus. Why on earth then does He come second, third, fourth, or even last on our list? Because we won't step aside in order to see Him glorified!

Does Jesus want us to serve? You better believe it. He tells us faith without works is dead. Does this mean we are saved by works? Absolutely not! "For by grace you have been saved through faith, and that not of yourselves; it is the gift of God" (Ephesians 2:8).

What it means is that a genuine heart of service must always and only flow out of an intimate relationship with Jesus. That intimate relationship will spark and equip us to be His vessel.

I had a bad habit of telling God what I planned to do each day and asking Him to bless it. That led to the distracted and troubled Martha style of serving. When I humbled myself before the King and allowed the Holy Spirit alone to lead my life, times of great and powerful service began to manifest.

If we desire to turn from the burdensome lifestyle of prideful service and want to receive from Him and be a servant that ministers from an overflow of intimacy with Him, a transition in authority must immediately take place. You and I must submit our lives under the authority and power of Jesus Christ and agree to let Him direct our every step. It does not matter what talents or gifts we think we possess. Without the Spirit of God, we will certainly fail.

Submitting to His authority sounds easy until we realize that we must submit in every single area of our lives. Not just in our jobs and churches, but in our thoughts, our desires, our visions, our dreams, and even with our children we must be submitted to Him.

What if Jesus told you He had never, including in all of Israel, seen faith like yours before? Would that encourage you? Consider the faithful lives included in the phrase "all of Israel." That would make us extremely joyful, wouldn't it? Look at the story of the centurion and his servant in Matthew 8:5-13:

> Now when Jesus had entered Capernaum, a centurion came to Him, pleading with Him, 6saying, "Lord, my servant is lying at home paralyzed, dreadfully tormented." 7And Jesus said to him, "I will come and heal him." 8The centurion answered and said, "Lord, I am not worthy that You should come under my roof. But only speak a word, and my servant will be healed. 9For I also am a man under

authority, having soldiers under me. And I say to this one, 'Go,' and he goes; and to another, 'Come,' and he comes; and to my servant, 'Do this,' and he does it.'" [10]When Jesus heard it, He marveled, and said to those who followed, "Assuredly, I say to you, I have not found such great faith, not even in Israel! [11]And I say to you that many will come from east and west, and sit down with Abraham, Isaac, and Jacob in the kingdom of heaven. [12]But the sons of the kingdom will be cast out into outer darkness. There will be weeping and gnashing of teeth." [13]Then Jesus said to the centurion, "Go your way; and as you have believed, so let it be done for you." And his servant was healed that same hour.

As the backbone of the Roman army, a centurion held a rank of great responsibility. We could compare his rank to that of a modern day sergeant major. In verse 10, Jesus recognized the faith of that man as the greatest He had seen.

Why? Was it because the centurion came to Jesus because he had a need? Maybe it was because he would not allow Jesus to come to his home because he felt unworthy. Yet, many people today express the same concerns. What then was it about the centurion soldier that impressed our Lord so much that He made such a significant and powerful statement? Here is how the Lord illuminated it to me in relation to authority.

First, in verse 8, he tells Jesus just to speak the word and it will be done. At that moment, the centurion revealed his heart regarding his thoughts on the reality of the power and authority that Jesus indeed possessed. He understood authority. Look at the next verse: he had soldiers under him, and when he said "come," they came. When he said "go," they went. When he said do something, people did it.

> WOULD YOU CHARACTERIZE YOUR LIFE AS A FOLLOWER OF JESUS CHRIST AS ONE THAT DAILY GETS TO SEE AND WITNESS EVENTS THAT GO FAR BEYOND THE REALM OF HUMAN POSSIBILITY?

The centurion knew what it was like to possess authority; but one problem surfaced. He was faced with a situation where he could not exercise his authority. His servant was ill, and no matter how much he ordered him to arise, the servant could not move.

What do you think that was like for that centurion? All of us can relate to possessing a measure of authority. As a boss, mother, father, sibling, or as socially independent, we all have authority to a certain degree. Why was the centurion considered more faithful than any that Jesus had yet encountered? One word could accurately describe it—submission. He, maybe for the first time in his career, had to place aside every power and ability that he possessed and trust the authority and power of Jesus Christ. Only through that degree of submission could the centurion witness an action beyond the realm of mere human capability.

Would you characterize your life as a follower of Jesus Christ as one that daily gets to see and witness events that go far beyond the realm of human possibility? If the answer is no, it may be because you do not fully submit to His leading and authority. The signs and wonders of Heaven should follow the lives of God's children everywhere they go. Why? The Holy Spirit who indwells the heart of believers desires to fill our lives and perform things through us that far surpass any authority we think we have alone.

Why do Christians today not see or experience the same miraculous power that was evident within the early church of Acts? The answer is quite simple. We are not submitting our entire authority to Christ and allowing Him control. God and His power certainly have not changed.

Ask yourself what areas of your life you have never surrendered and submitted to the authority of God. Your job, children, hobbies, spouse, and ministry all belong to Him. If you are not witnessing the supernatural in these areas of your life, perhaps you have not agreed to submit under His ability. One of the greatest errors in the life of a Christian is the refusal to submit fully under the authority of Christ our Lord.

There are so many areas of our lives that we seek to

> SURRENDER AND SUBMISSION ARE NOT YOU AND ME GIVING SOMETHING UP AS MUCH AS THEY ARE US RECEIVING DIVINE ASSISTANCE.

command and control, yet God instructs clearly that He should be our guide and leader. The centurion certainly operated with great command, but not until he went under the authority of a greater commander—Jesus—did he witness true power.

To some readers, the idea of surrendering all areas of our lives may seem extreme. Consider this: At some point in time, you and I will surrender and submit to Him regardless of whether or not we are ready. You may feel as if you do not need to surrender your vocation to Him because you have it all under control. But what happens when that job is stripped from you and you desperately need Him?

We feel at times that we can handle our family situations alone. What happens if illness strikes and our power is useless? Christ, at that point, will be the only authority capable of rescuing us.

God's ways are perfect. He sees the entire picture. We see here and now. Who do you think has the best chance of making correct decisions? Surrender and submission are not you and me giving something up as much as they are us receiving divine assistance. When we dedicate our homes, families, jobs, and ministries to the Lord, we do not lose them. Rather, those areas of our lives become enriched by the presence of the Lord, and we Christians begin to see the miraculous take place.

Know today that you, _____, (your name) are loved; you are special; you are redeemed; and you were specifically created for a purpose. You are gifted and equipped by the Creator to change this world for Jesus Christ. Yes, you!

CHAPTER SIX
Don't Move Without It

In light of the previous chapter, I considered how difficult it could be to walk daily submitting all our actions and decisions to the Lord. Certainly one could get extreme with that truth and struggle to make simple, everyday choices. If we resort to that sort of thought process, it appears we would be approaching the opposite end of the spectrum because when it comes to submission we would be placing intense pressure on ourselves to make decisions.

Here is the conclusion that I came to as I worked through many of these thoughts: This is not a formula but a legitimate Biblical principal. If we will seek daily to walk in and saturate our lives with the presence of the Lord, He will direct our every step.

I have spent seasons of life so worried about a decision I had to make that I became distracted and disconnected from my relationship with the Lord. It was not usually over things like where to eat lunch, but was over what job to accept or reject and things of that nature. I honestly thought that if I made the wrong decision over where to minister, God was going to completely disown me.

Let me pause here to clarify. I do not believe for a minute that Christians can pick and choose what they want to do and say they are in God's will because what they are doing is a "ministry." I firmly believe God has a unique and specific purpose for everyone and that we all must diligently seek His heart for direction in all matters.

My heart here is simply to demonstrate that a follower of Christ must seek faithfully to be consumed with the presence of the Lord. In doing this, we will relieve ourselves of the pressures of this world which hinder us as witnesses for Him. This is not to say that many decisions will not remain tough and require leaps of faith. Despite the importance or size of the choice that must be made, God's presence in your life will always lead to truth. Here is a brief example:

I am in a constant state of prayer prior to speaking to an audience concerning the appropriate message I am to share. I only desire to release what God's heart wants to release. Several months ago while preaching at a church pastored by my closest friend, the Lord tossed a curve ball and told me to change the message seconds before I was announced to come forward.

If you are a speaker or minister, you know how valuable it is to have notes and to be fresh concerning your knowledge of a sermon. My flesh wanted nothing more than to preach the message that I had prepared. I knew if I spoke on a topic that was not immediately familiar, I might look like an idiot. Well, since obedience is better than sacrifice, I heeded God's voice and spoke what the Lord said. And do you know what happened? Nothing!

Several weeks later, however, God allowed me to see a slight glimpse of His purpose for that last minute shift. While working at our family furniture store, I noticed two ladies from the church I previously mentioned looking around. One went on her way shopping while the other came to say hello to me. With tears welling up in her eyes, she confessed that the Lord had prepared that sermon specifically for her. It obviously impacted her life in a powerful way since she testified with such emotion weeks after the message. God did not need my vain and empty opinion. He needed obedience.

At any given moment, our lives can take a serious shift. That can happen personally or to an entire civilization. The stability we have experienced the last forty years in the nation in which we live may not continue. Regardless of our situation, the single most important aspect of a Christian's life is to remain in a constant saturation of the presence of the Lord. That presence represents truth, security, guidance, and love like none other. Do not live without it!

Have you ever wondered what it must have been like for

Moses as he led God's children through the wilderness in pursuit of the Promised Land? Difficult probably does not even begin to describe the anguish and distress he faced as a leader. We today are not unlike the faithful heroes of Bible history. They hurt. They cried. They experienced blessings and deliverance just like we do today.

So what set Moses apart? Turn to Exodus 33:15:

> Then he said to Him, "If your Presence does not
> go with us, do not bring us up from here ..."

What set Moses apart was simply this: he acknowledged and submitted to the fact that he was capable of nothing without the presence of the Lord. Look at what he says. Basically, "Lord, if Your presence does not go with me, I DO NOT WANT TO MOVE!" This is the heart cry of a man who knows he will not survive if the Lord is not present. The children of Israel grumbled, complained, and questioned his leadership. In summary, those people drove him crazy! His life and his calling did not appear to go quite as Moses had envisioned.

Look at the previous sequence of events:

➤ Exodus 24 – Moses has a meeting and abides in the glory of the Lord on Mount Sinai several days.

➤ Exodus 25 -31 – The Lord gives in precise detail how Moses is to construct the tabernacle. Take time to read this and analyze the details. God was very specific and enthusiastic about dwelling among His people. He loves all of His children so very much. Do we reciprocate? Keep reading. The next part will break your heart.

➤ Exodus 32 – While God converses with Moses concerning the details of the tabernacle, His children completely turn their faces from Him. Really let that soak in, Christian. At the very same moment God released the blueprints for His tabernacle, His children abandoned Him. Idolatry crept into the camp because there was no dedication or perseverance to the ways of the Lord.

It is easy to see why Moses was so adamant about walking in the presence of the Lord. He constantly found himself in situations where his capabilities were simply inadequate. Only through the leading of the Lord was victory possible.

Despite our every effort to do it on our own, we, like Moses, must understand that His presence is essential. That is precisely what set Moses apart as a servant of the Lord. The same will be true for us.

Can you relate to any seasons like that in your life? Each person reading this book has at least a small grasp of what it means to hurt. Many of you can relate to severe hurt. The only source of rescue and strength comes from saturating yourself in the presence of the Lord.

Moses knew he could not contend with those people. In a matter of days, they had broken the heart of the Lord and turned to idolatry. That indeed proved to be a difficult circumstance for Moses. His response: "Lord, I will follow, but only **where** Your presence goes do I want to go; and only **when** Your presence goes do I want to go."

What is it about the presence of the Lord that is so powerful? It is the act and commitment of daily saturating yourself with Him. When you are constantly filling yourself with the Holy Spirit of God, His divine character begins to rule, control, and lead your life.

For example, I am certain the average person has no idea how influential music is to a life. When one warms up for a sporting event, they play fast motivational music. Babies fall asleep to the sweet sound of a lullaby. Some couples dine to a romantic background melody. Likewise, crime, depression, anger, rebellion, and so much more have been scientifically linked to music. Why? Because what a person fills his or her life with will always manifest itself in the actions and character of that person.

> WHEN YOU ARE CONSTANTLY FILLING YOURSELF WITH THE HOLY SPIRIT OF GOD, HIS DIVINE CHARACTER BEGINS TO RULE, CONTROL, AND LEAD YOUR LIFE.

Let's be real here for a moment. We can all agree that something, whether a person, place, or thing, will consume and fill our lives. Occupation, family, sports—these and many other things leave us empty and unfulfilled because they are inadequate lovers. Saturation in the presence of the

Lord guarantees a character fashioned after that of Jesus Christ. He is a lover that cannot be overtaken or found guilty of let down.

What kind of season does this book find you in at this moment? How critical is the presence of the Lord to your current dilemma or trial?

One of the most sought after conditions of the human mind and body is the comfort and peace associated with rest. Many of us today are so troubled and consumed trying to survive that genuine rest and peace of mind seem impossible. If you are like me, you try many different ways to achieve the rest and comfort you desire, only to find further exhaustion.

Moses greatly needed rest. God gave Him the answer in Exodus 33:14: "My presence will go with you, and I will give you rest." The presence of the Lord truly rejuvenates and rekindles the heart.

Glance at Psalm 119 (KJV):

> 25My soul cleaveth unto the dust: **quicken** thou me according to thy word.

> 37Turn away mine eyes from beholding vanity; and **quicken** thou me in thy way.

> 40Behold, I have longed after thy precepts: **quicken** me in thy righteousness.

> 50This is my comfort in my affliction: for thy word hath **quickened** me.

[88]**Quicken** me after thy lovingkindness; so shall I keep the testimony of thy mouth.

[93]I will never forget thy precepts: for with them thou hast **quickened** me.

[107]I am afflicted very much: **quicken** me, O LORD, according unto thy word.

[149]Hear my voice according unto thy lovingkindness: O LORD, **quicken** me according to thy judgment.

[154]Plead my cause, and deliver me: **quicken** me according to thy word.

[156]Great are thy tender mercies, O LORD: **quicken** me according to thy judgments.

[159]Consider how I love thy precepts: **quicken** me, O LORD, according to thy lovingkindness.

There is nothing like His presence. It can genuinely bring a hurting and withered soul back to life. The Holy Spirit will breathe life into a weak vessel and literally quicken the dead. I love the Old English verb *quicken* as it emphasizes the act of making something alive. It is REVIVAL of the heart.

God is interested in and in love with you. Ask yourself, "Am I as close to Jesus Christ as I have ever been in my Christian life?" If not, why?

It does not matter how beat up or discouraged you feel. It does not matter how the world around you may appear. It may seem as if your world is falling apart. It may seem as if our nation is dissipating right before your eyes. You may feel as weak and incapable as you have ever felt in your entire life.

God can and will make you ALIVE again. He has a purpose and plan for your life that will indeed blow your mind and the minds of all those around you. It may or may not involve corporate success. It may or may not involve being popular. But if you keep your heart in submission to the heart of the Lord and abide in His pres-

> WE WOULD DIE TO GUARD OUR FAMILIES AND PROTECT OUR HOMES, BUT HOW HARD DO WE GUARD AND PROTECT OUR RELATIONSHIP WITH JESUS CHRIST?

ence, you will live a fulfilling life both personally and for the Kingdom of God.

For the sake of practicality and application, I will now offer the most basic description of abiding in the presence of the Lord. **Fall more in love with Jesus with each passing moment of each passing day—nothing more and nothing less**.

Think of it like this: Why do you want to be around or in the presence of a friend, girlfriend, boyfriend, spouse, child, etc.? You love them. Because of your strong love for them, many other aspects of your life become a part of their lives. Why not apply that same concept to your relationship with Jesus Christ? Don't worry about terminology such as "presence of the Lord." Don't worry about what you can do for Him. Don't worry about your theology or your philosophy.

Just worry about loving Jesus more. Everything else will flow out of that intimate relationship.

What are some things you would fight over or guard with all your heart and might? The natural response to that question might include family, home, money, cars, reputation, jobs, ministry, or social status. We would die to guard our families and protect our homes, but how hard do we guard and protect our relationship with Jesus Christ? Brother and Sister, let me be the first to confess that was me. I worked hard to guard my reputation. I worked even harder to guard my ministry, sometimes even putting it ahead of my family. In the midst of all the busyness and distraction I lost sight of intimacy with my Father.

For years and years, I did nothing to guard what I knew was the most important aspect of my entire being. God received second, third, and fourth place in my life. That was clearly idolatry!

We can be very critical of the children of Israel—look how fast they turned to idolatry. If there is something taking first place in your life, please know this: that position belongs to the Lord, and you are guilty of idolatry.

Idolatry became real to me not very long ago. In order for my family and me to guard our relationship with our Savior, we packed our bags and left our home, families, jobs, and ministries, driving 1,400 miles to the place where God instructed us to go for intimate communion with Him.

Never before had I made a commitment such as that, but my relationship with my Lord had taken a big hit. In the midst of ministry, work, and schooling floundered a broken spirit who neglected to protect the most sacred areas of his life. As I sit here writing, one month into this journey, I can tell you that the Lord has honored our obedience far beyond what we ever imagined.

I encourage you now as a brother with experience; do what you need to do as an individual or family to guard your relationship with Jesus Christ. If you fall back into His arms, He will not let you go. Take time now to pray and ask God for wisdom and discernment. He has a plan for you and your family and you will find it by sitting at His feet.

On several occasions during His earthly ministry, Jesus left the crowds to be alone with His Father. If intimacy with God was critical to His own Son, how much more essential is it to the lives of believers today? Do we guard our intimacy with God above all else? So many times we have no idea what the Lord is trying to say to us simply because we do not spend enough time with Him to actually be familiar with His voice. Consider these verses:

➢ Luke 6:12-13 – Before assembling and selecting the twelve disciples, Jesus withdrew Himself from the action to hear the voice of His Father.

➢ Matthew 26:36-46 – Prior to His arrest and persecution, Jesus was in the garden intensely seeking the voice of His Father.

➢ Luke 9:28-29 – Jesus led Peter, John, and James to the mountain to pray, and His entire countenance was altered.

The very Son of God, equipped with authority and power directly from God, faithfully dismissed Himself from situations so that He could hear the voice of His Father. Even amidst great healings, wonders, and large crowds, Jesus departed to a place of solitude for one purpose alone: submission through intimacy.

Despite endless capabilities, the Son of God only did what His Father asked Him to do:

> Then Jesus answered and said to them, "Most assuredly, I say to you, the Son can do nothing of Himself, but what He sees the Father do; for whatever He does, the Son also does in like manner.
>
> —John 5:19

Jesus submitted all the power He possessed under the authority of God. He went where His Father sent Him. He spoke what the Father wanted Him to speak. He healed only whom the Father desired Him to heal. He suffered and died for the sins of mankind. Jesus submitted to His Father's will—period. He remained obedient because of intentional intimacy.

Submission begins with intimacy. Jesus literally battled to be alone with the Lord. Do you guard your relationship with Him more than any other factor in your life? If it is submission you seek, you have to find a way to answer that question with a "yes!"

CHAPTER SEVEN
Bearers of Truth

The subtitle of this book is "Heeding Only His Voice" because the story of the Good Shepherd is my favorite passage of Scripture. John 10 is full of encouragement, instruction, warning, and promise—all of which significantly impact the life of a follower of Christ. Although this passage is not designed to be the focus for this particular chapter, it lays a solid foundation for the topic we will examine.

Did you realize that sheep are considered to be the dumbest animals on the face of the planet? In addition to their inability to learn or follow directions, they are also very stubborn creatures. If they get too far from the fold (just a few yards away), they feel lost. If they fall on their sides, they cannot get up. Without the full guidance of a shepherd, a sheep cannot eat, travel, or survive.

Mankind, on the other hand, is a knowledgeable species. Humans are capable of survival and prosperity without much outside assistance. Despite the vast differences that exist between man and sheep, sheep have a firm grasp on a principle every believer in the world desperately needs. They follow only one voice.

John 10:4-5 reveals two things:

➢ Sheep heed the voice of their shepherd.

➢ Sheep flee from unknown voices.

While sheep may not be able to feed, defend, or provide for themselves, this humble, stubborn, and ignorant species has perfected the art of pure obedience and submission to their shepherd.

In a given day, we have literally hundreds and hundreds of different voices trying to influence us. By "voices" I mean all kinds of persuasion and enticement that will either lead us towards the Lord or away from Him. In every case except for the voice of God, those pulls are direct lies and devices of the enemy, or as is detected in John 10:8, the "thieves and robbers." Today can be the day that we refuse and rebuke the lies of the enemy and cling only to the truth that proceeds from the voice of the Good Shepherd.

God's Word is clear concerning the power of the tongue. A lie wreaks devastation. Lies destroy people's character and their attitudes about themselves, their families, their relationships, the church, etc.

What makes a lie so detrimental is that it speaks into ex-istence false and negative implications that are contrary to the truth of the Scriptures. Because those implications are contrary to the Word, they do not nor will they ever provide life or edification.

If you do not think lies are a serious issue, pray and con-sider asking God why it is listed in Proverbs 6 among the seven things He hates. Simply stated, accepting the lies of the enemy is deadly to you and those around you.

For the sake of highlighting and illustrating the negative influence that lies have over a life, I want to try something. Think of these lies that we often succumb to: You are des-tined for failure, and you will never amount to anything. You will never be able to break those addictions. You will always be depressed and will never experience true joy. Your marriage and your relationship with your children will fail. You will never be used by God; you are too unworthy. Your church can't spark revival; it is too small. You can't make an impact; you are a woman. You can't make a difference; you are too young.

As you read those words, how did they make you feel? Depending on which ones applied directly to you, feelings of discouragement, fear, failure, defeat, and bitterness probably welled up within you. I spoke about this in a church once and trust me, it was as quiet as a mouse and faces froze. Hearing these lies instantly brought defeat to the ears. Try repeating them aloud if at first they did not devastate your heart.

On the other hand, what does truth sound like? It sounds like life: You are a child of the Most High God. He has divinely created you for a purpose. You will prevail in and under the name of Christ. Your marriage and your family will prevail and prosper for the sake of His kingdom. You can reach the world despite your race, gender, or age. You will be free and experience a life of peace and joy that all of mankind will desire. God will use you to set the captives free. You are His son or daughter, and He will never leave your side. Those truths generate an entirely different set of emotions within the mind and body.

Certainly this is not about emotional feelings, nor is it about prosperity or a "name it and claim it" philosophy. This is about speaking life and truth from the Word of God into a heart and watching it grow. Sure, the list just mentioned is meant for Christians. (If you are not a Christian reading this, let me assure you that God loves you very much. He sent His Son, Jesus Christ to die in your place for the sins that you have committed. Salvation is freely available to all who will answer the call of Jesus Christ on their lives. If this is you, please turn to Appendix A and read more. This is the greatest possible decision a person could ever make!)

> YOU HAVE BECOME CAPABLE OF PERFORMING THINGS THAT WILL ALTER LIVES AND GENERATIONS TO COME.

Satan loves nothing more than to offer lies to the hearts

and minds of God's people to hinder or discourage their efforts to know Him. The truth is: God has an incredible plan for the lives of those who submit fully to Him.

When you submit your life fully under the authority of Jesus Christ, the enemy begins to get seriously concerned. Why? As a humble, obedient servant who abides in the secret place, you have become capable of performing things that will alter lives and generations to come. God will use you to set captives free and bring salvation to entire households. Satan hates this, and he will lie to you and try to trick you into believing things about yourself or other people that are not truth.

If you are a young man or woman, boy or girl reading this book, the enemy might be trying to tell you that you are too young and inexperienced to be effective for furthering the Kingdom of God. He may try to tell you that your voice is of no significance and that nobody is going to hear what you have to say. Do not believe those lies. God has ordained and called you to be His man or woman on the scene, and if you remain a willing and humble vessel, He will put His words in your mouth just like He did for Jeremiah.

Maybe you are a follower of Christ who has been bombarded with the lie that because of who you are and where you came from God could not possibly work through your life. Whether it is your past or your heritage, you feel as if you do not measure up to the caliber of a person that God could use for mighty miracles.

Please, read Judges 6 and 7. Gideon was the least in a

family that was at the bottom of the social class. However, because he was an obedient and humble vessel, God used him and a mere 300 soldiers to wipe out 135,000 Midianites. If you do the math, you will see that he faced odds of about 450 to 1. Did you catch that as you read? That means that every one of Gideon's soldiers had to withstand 450 Midianites. I guarantee you that at the beginning of that journey Gideon never would have imagined that God could use His life for such a purpose. The truth is: God will do the same for us.

Some reading this book may struggle from severe insecurities—physical or emotional. Do not believe the lies of the enemy concerning your life or your body. You are a child of the King, one adopted into the royal priesthood. If the enemy is consuming your mind with thoughts of fear or failure or inadequacies, stand firm and combat them with the Word of God. Anything that this world seeks to offer you about yourself that appears contrary to the character and love of the Holy Spirit is not from Him. Fight those lies with Scripture.

I have a quote by Pastor Adam Meisberger written in my Bible that penetrates my heart like a knife every time I read it: "The greatest lie offered to Christians from the enemy is that we are weak and powerless." That could not be more accurately spoken.

How many Christians today walk through their everyday lives with a defeated mentality? I am just as guilty as the next person. Either we don't care because we are bombarded with distractions, or we don't feel equipped because we succumb to the lies of the enemy. Regardless, we are missing chances every single day to see miracles and changed lives. You and I don't need to question the promises of the One who is incapable of telling a lie.

Look to Numbers 13 and 14 for some serious warnings and encouragements relating to falling subject to the lies of the enemy. Please place this book aside, pick up the Scriptures, and diligently seek God for answers within your heart. Ask Him to reveal areas in your life where you have been captive to the lies of the enemy. Ask Him to equip you with verses of promise that will forever remove those plagues from your life. If your calling and your destiny are being compromised due to lies, it is essential that you recognize them and rebuke them immediately.

> "THE GREATEST LIE OFFERED TO CHRISTIANS FROM THE ENEMY IS THAT WE ARE WEAK AND POWERLESS."
>
> -PASTOR ADAM MEISBERGER

First, read aloud the names of the twelve spies mentioned in verses 4-16 of chapter 13. **The spies were as follows: Shammua, Shaphat, Caleb, Igal, Joshua, Palti, Gaddiel, Gaddi, Ammiel, Sethur, Nahbi, and Geuel.** If you are like most readers, it is quite possible that the only names you recognized were Joshua and Caleb. Why? They were the only bearers of truth.

When sending those twelve men to Canaan to spy out the land, Moses gave them specific assignments. In Numbers 13:18-20, we see he wanted them to find out who was living there, what they were like, how strong they appeared, what the land was like, and what the vegetation rendered.

Before we continue, let me ask you a very deep question. What do the words "Promised Land" imply? My guess would be a land that was promised to them.

In other words, it did not really matter what they were about to see because it was territory that already belonged to them. And maybe that is why God wanted them to go and spy it out. So their faith could be strengthened knowing that despite the apparent opposition, their God was much mightier than the enemy. What happened next within the hearts of the ten spies is also a pandemic today within the Body of Christ, and it saddens our Lord.

In Numbers 14: 26-33, the heartbreak unfolds. Within the realm of those few verses, we witness ten men making a decision to deny the promise of God to all His children and falling victim to the lies of the enemy. Listen to the tone and descriptions of their discoveries. Verse 32 directly states that the ten spies brought back an evil report. In verse 33 they even went so far as to refer to themselves as mere grasshoppers in the presence of the giants of Anak. Does the dialogue recorded in those few verses reflect a group of men who truly believed that land had already been promised to them? They journeyed to a land of promise, received a lie, and spoke a lie, and we are witnesses of the tragic consequences it brought on the entire camp.

As you read Numbers 14, observe carefully what takes place. This should stand as a strong warning to all Christians against deception of the heart, mind, and spirit. Verses 1-2 reveal that the entire camp cried and wept in discouragement because of the news they received. They also reveal that the children began to murmur against Moses and Aaron and to verbally question God's sovereign guidance. Our great God had just delivered them from bondage under Pharaoh in Egypt. Did you catch that? While in Egypt they were all in bondage. Now, they were free individuals on a journey to a land of promise but were suffering major setbacks because they wouldn't believe the truth. Be careful about judging. You and I are not much different. Verse 4 is perhaps the most heartbreaking passage in the entire story and accurately depicts the end result of lives that refuse the truth and becomes subject to lies:

> So they said to one another, "Let us select a leader
> and return to Egypt."
>
> —Numbers 14:4

That's right; they were so discouraged, confused, and defeated they desired to select a new commander and return to the land of bondage.

How tragic are the wicked devices of the enemy. They can cause you to lose sight of your promised land and send you on a journey straight back into the bondage that gripped your life before you came to Jesus Christ. You do not have to receive that! Where were Joshua and Caleb when the evil report occurred? They were refuting those lies with truth and keeping their focus on the promise. Numbers 13:30 says that Caleb tried to calm the people by assuring them that God would give them strength. Numbers 14:6-9 says that Joshua and Caleb were in distress and continued to plead the truth. They could have kept silent, but they did not.

Speak out, Christian! Whether it is personally or within your family, church, or community, do not let the lies sneak in and destroy what God's Word promises. You have the authority, with a heart of humility and love, to rebuke lies every time you hear them.

Many times it will cost you. Numbers 14:10 shows the people wanted to stone Joshua and Caleb for defending the truth. What happened? God came to their rescue. Be a bearer of truth within your life and within the lives around you and watch God show up every single time. The enemy wants nothing more than to beat you up and kill you spiritually—and he does it with mind games. Believing lies will cost you, but remember you do not have to receive them.

Think back to that first list of names and the fact that you recognized only two. The reason you never heard of the other ten spies is explained in Numbers 14:36-38: They were destroyed.

I am not going to trivialize the severity of lies and what believing them can do to your life physically and spiritually, but I want to encourage you. No matter how defeated you feel at this moment, God does not want to destroy you. He wants to give you the chance to run to His promises. If you deny His voice, there will be consequences. Verbally rebuke and deny the lies you know are restricting your walk and your faith in Him. If God says you can—regardless of what the enemy may tell you—you can. You can be healed. You can be delivered. You can be used by God. You can be free to walk steadfastly towards your promised land.

Never forget that the same Spirit that raised Jesus Christ from the dead desires to fully indwell and lead every area of your life. If you have accepted Him as Savior, you have access to literally thousands of verses and promises to lead and guide you. Any other voice should immediately be identified as a thief and a robber who only has one goal: to rob you from intimacy with your Good Shepherd. When that happens to sheep, the dumbest animals on the planet, they don't sit there and decipher what should be done; they run from that voice.

Brothers and Sisters, the devil wants to destroy your life, and he will seek to do that in the most subtle ways. His finest and filthiest craft is deception. He will lie to you, trick you, and divert you from the truth if you sit and listen to his lies.

May we, advanced and technologically driven mankind, take a lesson from the lowly sheep. Run from the strange voices. Cling and submit only to the voice of our Shepherd Jesus Christ. Will you believe God and His Word or be stifled by the nasty serpent? In these final days, we need to live each day with reckless abandonment for Christ.

Write out promises from God's Word that will help you fight lies that plague your life. Use a Bible and concordance to help you locate verses that speak to your particular struggles. For example, if you feel unworthy of God's love, find verses that talk about His love and how He made a great sacrifice for you. If you struggle with fear, locate and record verses that display the protection and safety you experience in the presence of Jesus Christ. First identify the struggles, and then investigate God's Word for answers.

_____
_____
_____
_____

One of the greatest lies that plague the members of the Body of Christ is the fear that hinders their tongues from releasing His words. I want to close this chapter with a story shared with our church by a Russian missionary. May this true account encourage you to be God's voice every time He calls.

After a powerful encounter with the Lord, a young Russian man gave his heart to Jesus. Following that miracle, he felt a strong call from the Father to preach the Gospel. He went to his pastor and asked permission to speak at a particular service. The young Russian sought counsel from his pastor because he was unsure about public speaking. The pastor faithfully encouraged him to rely solely on the Holy Spirit for guidance.

The time finally arrived, and the Russian lad was nervous beyond what he had ever experienced before. A few ministers spoke to him prior to his message, which heightened his anxiety. His pastor introduced him, and he approached the stage with much reservation. He gazed out at the audience for several moments. An atmosphere of confusion and expectation flowed through the audience. All, including the pastor, had no idea what was about to hit them.

The Scriptures, the pastor, and other faithful servants had instructed him to open his mouth and allow the Lord to speak. That is exactly what this Russian brother was about to do. He looked intently into the heart of the audience, opened his mouth, and shouted the word CABBAGE!

Unsure of what to do next amidst the awkward silence that filled the room, the young man began to close in prayer. (My wife thinks I am crazy, but I cry each time I get to this part.) Just as he was about to step down after concluding his brief and peculiar sermon, a faint sound was heard from the back corner of the church house. The audience stared as a man rose from his seat, walked down the aisle, and surrendered his heart to Christ at the altar.

Needless to say, the pastor was intrigued by the miracle that God had just performed. He learned that all week the young Russian preacher had practiced his sermons while laboring in the cabbage fields. He had shouted out the Word of God throughout the day. The gentleman in the pew was a thief who had also been in that cabbage field—for different reasons of course. All week he had heard this strange man shouting out messages of hope and redemption through Jesus Christ. When he heard the young Russian minister speak the word CABBAGE from the altar, he knew God was calling his name.

God did not need a fancy detailed message to reach that

soul. He needed an obedient, humble messenger. Consider this in relation to the story. Despite your capabilities to preach, minister, witness, counsel, or lead, lives will not change without the power of the Holy Spirit. Ask yourself this question. Do I implement my capabilities more than I operate in obedience? Life changing power is found through submission—period.

CHAPTER EIGHT
Inadequate Armor

Transformation often fails to occur because we Christians will not allow our hearts to break for that which breaks the heart of Jesus Christ. With this thought in mind, consider carefully this statement: Our security in ourselves, our finances, our families, our institutions, and our economy hinders our submission to Almighty God. Most Christians would agree verbally that true security only exists within the authority and love of Christ Jesus. However, the action which must follow that verbal acknowledgement is seriously lacking.

When we submit to the authority and leading of Christ, it means laying aside our security or armor. Does this mean we have to give away everything we own or refuse to visit a doctor or receive medicine again? "No." What it means, however, is that within the innermost parts of our hearts, we know and acknowledge that the Lord Jesus Christ is our supplier, provider, protector, and armor. If He says give away all our money, we do not question it. If He asks us to step away from some of the securities we hold to, we should not be inclined to resist. This may sound easy, and we may even think we can keep our securities as long as Jesus is first.

One problem: it is going to be hard to exemplify a life of submission to Jesus Christ when on the outside there appear to be no areas where we fully rely upon God. Man's security always leads to a lack of submission to God. If you think that is bold, opinionated, and inaccurate, consider the life of every single servant of God recorded in the pages of Scripture. Consider also the present day biographies and testimonies of men and women who surrendered the comforts of this world so that Christ could be exalted. Why? When our security is surrendered, any and all authority we actually thought we possessed is surrendered as well. Therefore, Christ's authority is exalted above worldly security so that when miracles do happen, only God can receive the glory.

This is why God knocked down the walls of Jericho with the sound of trumpets. Certainly Joshua and his men would have been more secure if they had at least possessed weapons with which to battle. But in such security, even if it is meager, we tend to rely a little less on God and a little more on ourselves. As worldly/human security increases, the dependence upon the Lord tends to decrease.

What makes this such a difficult truth to apply revolves

around the fact that we as Americans have tasted security and have come to find satisfaction in it. All the while, our faith and submission to the desires and plans of our Heavenly Father suffer compromise. This idea of decreasing our human security to increase in our submission is not a matter of opinion.

Consider the result of the situation with Joshua and the taking down of the walls of Jericho. He had to relinquish all his preconceived ideas of how it should be done and trust the leading of the Lord. If Joshua and his men had not decreased, God could not have increased. It is all about submission.

The classic example of someone relinquishing all security in the heat of the battle is the giant-slaying shepherd boy named David. Picture Goliath, all of nine-feet-something, marching to and fro with well over 100 pounds of armor strapped to his body. The entire Israeli army was petrified of what that giant might do to any challenger

> WHEN OUR SECURITY IS SURRENDERED, ANY AND ALL AUTHORITY WE ACTUALLY THOUGHT WE POSSESSED IS SURRENDERED AS WELL.

who dared to step in his path. David, looking to provide his brothers with some food, approached the battle ground and heard the roar of the giant all through the valley. The men of Israel fled, but David approached Saul and said, "Do not fear, I will fight him" (I Samuel 17:32).

David, of course, was immediately rebuked. He was just a

young, inexperienced shepherd boy. Read David's very powerful and faithful rebuttal to Saul's negative words:

> But David said to Saul, "Your servant used to keep
> his father's sheep, and when a lion or a bear came
> and took a lamb out of the flock, [35]I went out after it
> and struck it, and delivered the lamb from its mouth;
> and when it arose against me, I caught it by its beard,
> and struck and killed it. [36]Your servant has killed
> both lion and bear; and this uncircumcised Philistine
> will be like one of them, seeing he has defied the
> armies of the living God." [37]Moreover, David said,
> "The LORD, who delivered me from the paw of the
> lion and from the paw of the bear, He will deliver me
> from the hand of this Philistine." And Saul said to
> David, "Go, and the LORD be with you!"
> —1 Samuel 17:34-37

David spoke up, "Listen here. I am not your average shepherd boy, for I am a servant of the Almighty God. A lion and
bear came and snatched a dear lamb from my father's fold,
and I went after that one. When the lion came after me, I
grabbed him by his beard and cut off his head. The same was
true for the bear because they came against one of my own.
The same will be true of this big uncircumcised Philistine
because he comes against my God."

I don't know about you, but that sounds like a powerful
resume to me. David had personal experience battling under
the authority of God. His security as he fought for the life of
a mere sheep was God and God alone.

Watch what happened in verses 38-39. Saul attempted to gird David with the necessary armor to withstand the battle. If I were Saul, I certainly would have done the same thing. Let's get real here: David was about to battle the largest most powerful man around. Certainly, he would need a sword and some protective gear to give him even the slightest chance of accidentally defeating this warrior.

My entire purpose for this chapter rests in verse 39. We must allow God to convict us and show us how to make this kind of submission a part of our everyday lives as His followers.

> David fastened his sword to his armor and tried to walk, for he had not tested them. And David said to Saul, "I cannot walk with these, for I have not tested them." So David took them off.
>
> —1 Samuel 17:39

Read the last sentence of verse 39 six or seven times. What did David do with the securities that man was offering to him? David put them off. David put them off. David put them off. And you know my friend? What a game-changer that decision was. David abandoned his abilities and skills, no matter how small or great they were, so God could reign and perform a miraculous work.

I will go ahead and tell you before you begin to wonder or find out the hard way—this world, your friends, your family, maybe even your church, will think you are crazy when you begin to operate under that level of submission. Finish reading the details about the battle with Goliath. Goliath mocked and belittled David as the little shepherd reached into his pouch and selected one of the five smooth stones he had previously chosen from a stream. Imagine how the Philistine army roared with laughter as some petite shepherd boy ran towards the most powerful warrior on the battle front with his sling whirling in the air.

Ponder and apply this information to your own life. There was David, face to face with a giant. Behind him were those too scared to submit and trust the authority of the living God. In front of him came nothing but laughter and mocking. David let neither side hinder his faith. Had he listened to the laughter, he would have quit. Had he listened to his companions, he would have failed by hiding behind human security. But by submitting to his Father in Heaven, David became the giant killer.

> THE SECURITIES THAT YOU NEED TO BE WILLING TO ABANDON ARE THE ONES THAT DIMINISH YOUR ABILITY TO FULLY RELY UPON GOD.

Ask the Lord to deal with your heart concerning areas where your security may indeed hinder your reliance and faith in Christ Jesus. Do you desire to be a giant slayer? Do you want God to take your life and use it in such a way that He can be glorified and this world left dumbfounded? Take those areas of security and like David, DROP THEM OFF!

Be transparent and obedient through this process, allowing

God to have full reign in the transformation of your heart. Remember, this will be a game changer. The securities that you need to be willing to abandon are the ones that diminish your ability to fully rely upon God. Does that mean you get rid of all our food or medicine? I hope you know that my heart is not legalistic or dogmatic about that in any way. God has indeed given us medicine, doctors, food, and clothes. But if you have a heart that genuinely desires to grow closer to the Lord, you will submit to His voice. He will then reveal to you the specific areas you need to surrender to Him.

Let's look at it like this: Someone could say, "David was not submitted and fully trusting in the Lord because he picked up a rock and a sling. Why didn't he just walk up to the giant and trust that the Lord would kill him?" David obeyed the voice and leading of God which directed him to drop off man's armor and approach the giant with a sling and a stone.

Likewise, God may reveal to you that you find too much security in your wealth and may command you to give some away in order that you may grow closer to Him. But that may not be the case for another. God may reveal to you that you find too much security in doctors as you battle through a certain illness, and He may ask you to step away from medicine and trust Him. But that may not be the case for the next person with medical needs. God may reveal to you that you find too much security in family, friends, jobs, money, church, or ministry—the list can go on and on and be very unique to each individual. Here is the main point of concern. When you get before God and He reveals what areas He needs you to submit, will you obey?

I received a phone call today from my friend, Leo, who shared a story with me about an encounter he had with a complete stranger. He told me that after looking into the eyes of the man, he knew God had set up a divine appointment, but because nothing spectacular immediately occurred, my friend got in his car and drove away.

The Lord immediately told him to turn around, go back, and place a certain amount of money in the man's hand. My friend obeyed, but still nothing observable appeared to happen. Once again, he left. As he drove down the interstate, he conversed with God about it. Here is a paraphrase of what God told him: "It was not about that man; it was about you operating in obedience. I don't need your money and neither did he, but I needed to see your obedience."

As we talked, I was reminded of times when I obeyed God's voice, only to be looked at as foolish. It dawned on me in that brief conversation that God was **only** looking for obedience. If God had sent my friend back just to give that man a big kiss on his forehead, as long as he obeyed, God would have been glorified.

This is a huge and essential step in your journey towards an authentically powerful relationship with the God of the Universe. Remember how we discussed David's release of security and how it was viewed by those around him? The Philistines laughed, and perhaps the Israelites doubted. Surrounding David was every possible temptation to abandon submission and cling to human security. Perhaps voices from behind him shouted, "What are you thinking, David? You will never make it without a sword and a shield." Perhaps voices in front of him shouted, "Run, you sissy. You will not last one measly second carrying that small stone!"

From every angle imaginable, you will be enticed with desires to hold on to that which makes logical sense to this world, even if it means disobeying the voice of God. This must not continue to happen. If your heart desires to draw closer and be used mightily of the Lord, the only thing that you can offer is complete obedience.

In relation to David's steadfast commitment to obey and fight for the Lord, he not only had to crucify and put off the security of manmade armor, but he had to rebuke and put off the insecurity that taunted him from the front. Remember, Goliath and the Philistines surely thought it comical to see the little shepherd approach with a sling and a stone. That rebuke and mocking could have led to insecurities which could have caused David to quit and abandon God's perfect plan in that moment of his life. Just as worldly security can hinder submission, insecurity can be equally devastating.

In both cases, security and insecurity tend to exist and survive only in an environment of pride and selfishness. If we are insecure to make a move of submission and obedience because of what others may think, then we place our own glory above God's. If we are so secure in our worldly abilities and possessions that we cannot be totally surrendered to God, then we place our own glory above God's. David had to deal with the laughter (insecurity) and David had to drop off the armor (security) which his comrades sought to provide him. Neither one stood in the way of David's submission and obedience to God. For that reason and that reason alone,

David slew a giant that day. He did the impossible because he obeyed God. It's all about submission.

What **securities** do you possess that hinder your ability to fully rely on God? As you receive an answer, consider if that security is worth missing out on what God truly has planned for your life. Receiving the armor would have compromised God's glory for that moment in David's life. That is why he put the armor off!

What **insecurities** hinder you from fully submitting to the plan of God in your life? As you receive an answer, consider if it is worth missing out on what God has planned for your life. Listening to the jeering and laughter of the Philistines would have compromised God's glory for that moment in David's life. He did not heed those voices which sought to divert him.

Many times, God will require you to do things that make no sense to anyone around you. Unfortunately, that makes following His voice that much more difficult at times. Once again, go to the Scriptures and investigate. Every authentic follower of Christ was used by God to perform tasks that looked and sounded absolutely foolish to this world: Noah building the ark, Abraham sacrificing his son Isaac, Gideon fighting with only 300 soldiers, Joshua sounding trumpets,

> MANY TIMES, GOD WILL REQUIRE YOU TO DO THINGS THAT MAKE NO SENSE TO ANYONE AROUND YOU.

Christ dying on the cross. The works of God often make no logical sense to this world.

So, here is the game-changing question for you and me as we seek to understand how to walk a life of constant obedience before the Lord: Will we relinquish our earthly securities so that we may be fully submitted to God and used by Him to impact the world for Jesus Christ? This world has some very enticing armor—money, fame, possessions. All those offer a sense of accomplishment, success, and authority. If we hide behind that armor, we may be deemed a great success by man, but we will never be giant slayers for the Kingdom.

If you are reading this book, God is obviously working and stirring within your heart. Lay down this book and fall on your face and ask Him to show you what to do next. He loves a heart that cries out and seeks His face, and He will surely hear your cry. He is your Daddy!

Achieving worldly security is usually presented in a step by step formula. If your desire is to be a simple but powerful tool of the Mighty Creator, there is only one step: Obedience. No matter how crazy or foolish it may seem, there is no sweeter aroma that reaches Heaven's throne than that which flows from the heart of a humble obedient child of God. You were put here to perform greatness through the power of the Holy Spirit. Don't settle for anything less!

CHAPTER NINE
He Didn't Accept It Then,
He Won't Accept It Now

In light of the information God released in the previous chapter, it is critical that we take action with our hearts and not merely our lips. Lip service is a spiritual condition God utterly rejects. It's not acceptable that we only know and acknowledge what we need to do. We must actively make our commitment and obedience to God an action of our hearts. Glancing back to David's battle with Goliath for a moment, we see a great example: Even though he knew God wanted him to battle with only a sling and a stone, the complete submission of David's heart did not occur until he put off the armor.

During the brief but powerful earthly ministry of Jesus Christ, He was constantly bombarded with rebuke and questions from men who were exceptionally knowledgeable of the Old Testament. Usually referred to as scribes and Pharisees, those men were committed students of the Torah and very learned in the Law. However, as we mentioned earlier in the story of the blind man, they were so blinded by error they could not see Jesus' love. They are an accurate description of a "lip service" follower of Christ. They knew what to say. They knew what they were supposed to do and not do, but outside a mere list of rules and regulations, there existed little or no love relationship with the Savior of the world.

Quietly and effectively, the enemy has infiltrated our churches and believers with that tragic mentality. Suddenly, the term Christian, which is truly a condition and transformation of the heart, has become a title given to those who do or practice certain rituals. That is devastating and heartbreaking to the heart of the Lord and has led to a serious demise in the spiritual condition of Christians in America and across the globe.

There are a few things I feel led to discuss as we continue but, not before presenting this passage to which the Lord wants to draw our attention:

> Then the scribes and Pharisees who were from Jerusalem came to Jesus, saying, "Why do Your disciples transgress the tradition of the elders? For they do not wash their hands when they eat bread."

³He answered and said to them, "Why do you also transgress the commandment of God because of your tradition? ⁴For God commanded, saying, 'Honor your father and your mother'; and, 'He who curses father or mother, let him be put to death. But you say, 'Whoever says to his father or mother, "Whatever profit you might have received from me is a gift to God"— ⁶then he need not honor his father or mother.' Thus you have made the commandment of God of no effect by your tradition. Hypocrites! Well did Isaiah prophesy about you, saying: ⁸' These people draw near to Me with their mouth, And honor Me with their lips, But their heart is far from Me. ⁹And in vain they worship Me, Teaching as doctrines the commandments of men.' ¹⁰When He had called the multitude to Himself, He said to them, "Hear and understand: ¹¹Not what goes into the mouth defiles a man; but what comes out of the mouth, this defiles a man.

—Matthew 15:1-11

> SUDDENLY, THE TERM CHRISTIAN, WHICH IS TRULY A CONDITION AND TRANSFORMATION OF THE HEART, HAS BECOME A TITLE GIVEN TO THOSE WHO DO OR PRACTICE CERTAIN RITUALS.

Did you catch what was presented in verses 1-2? Jesus and his disciples were challenged because they did not wash their hands before they ate. Notice what the Pharisees consider that: a "transgression." Their tradition held that the hands must be sprinkled with water before taking bread. While that may be a good custom for the sake of cleanliness, it was not a commandment. Unfortunately, to some with that attitude, violating a custom, tradition, or doctrine was worse than violating God's Word. In the worst of situations, the tradition may have even contradicted God's Word. Jesus instantly rebuked their argument in verses 3-6 as He revealed their fault of placing tradition ahead of such commands as honoring their fathers and mothers.

Jesus, well aware of the Pharisee's knowledge of the Scriptures, readily quoted from the Old Testament. In that manner, He could effectively demonstrate the difference between knowing what to do and actually putting it to action. Jesus quoted Isaiah 29:13 as He proclaimed in verses 7-8: "Hypocrites! Well did Isaiah prophesy about you, saying: 'These people draw near to Me with their mouth, And honor Me with their lips, But their heart is far from Me.'" That silenced the Pharisees.

I have read that verse many times in my life and have felt as if that prophecy from the book of Isaiah was for me. For many years, I possessed a form of godliness but with my life denied the power of Jesus. I knew what to say and what not to say. I knew what to do and what not to do. All the while, my so-called Christian life was nothing more than a mere lip-serving, man-pleasing theology that contained little regard for intimacy with my Jesus.

Carefully consider verse 9: "In vain they do worship me, teaching for doctrine the commandments of men." In other words, a life of lip service is meaningless and unfruitful. We as humans can fool anybody. We cannot fool God.

And I love that rebuke of their theology, "teaching for doctrines the commandments of men." That is another costly error that has caused much grief within the Body of Christ. When rituals or manmade traditions replace the authentic working of the Holy Spirit, there is no chance of survival. For centuries fellow brothers and sisters have argued tradition and treated it as doctrine. Matters relating to music style, clothing, orders of worship, and other such cultural issues have accomplished the heartbreaking act of dividing the Body of Christ.

I firmly believe that we must hold unyieldingly—without compromise—to the Holy Word of God. Certain doctrines cannot be questioned under any circumstance. But what I am speaking about here is the lip service practice that allows tradition to be presented as doctrine. That has caused great devastation to the church worldwide. It has shifted people's thinking from Christ to denomination and has caused a society of believers to become focused on their kingdom and not His.

What does Scripture say about division? It weakens. The tradition of man has resulted in dozens of Christian denominations all claiming faith and hope in the same Savior but disconnected from one another: "They worship contemporary," or "they take communion every week," or "they don't do two songs before they preach," or "they don't dress very nicely." How long will this sort of ignorance hinder the full power of the Body of Christ? It is time we submit as a body to the Holy Spirit and place our traditions aside. A heart that longs to see Christ lifted high must break free from this suffocating predicament.

What is tradition of man but the opinion of a sinful, imperfect human? I have sat in a service where an evangelist rebuked someone for the act of leading music with a shirt and tie that did not match well together. I have seen ministers look down on other ministers because they did not preach in a full blown suit. That is pure opinion! That is teaching the commandment of man as authority and doctrine.

Will the Holy Spirit not speak through a man who does not have a piece of fabric hanging from his neck? Actually, that would imply that every minister in a third world country who had to preach in a tunic or old pair of slacks was not worthy. Do you see my point? That mentality is not Scriptural, nor does it edify the Body.

Legalism of that sort seeks to minimize the power of God and elevate the wisdom of man. A heart surrendered to the Lord remains sensitive and obedient to the Holy Spirit rather than to a rule or a formality. The Pharisees proclaimed the importance of washing the hands. Jesus announced the importance of washing the heart. What are you going to do with what God reveals to you as you seek His face? Lip service is accepted by man but utterly rejected by God.

The primary problem with lip service is that it is man seeking to please and glorify his fellow men. It does not represent a heart that seeks to obey and please only God. Notice what Jesus says in verse 9 about the worship and teaching of a person who seeks to please mankind rather than God. He says all of their efforts and labors are in vain. One may ask: "Why is this issue so critical? At least lip-service Christians are doing good things." Let's reference a verse from Isaiah 42:8: "He will not share His glory." Lip service only glorifies man. Heart service glorifies God.

I can think of several stories to share at this time, but I always find that God's lessons presented through His Word are better. Matthew 21:28-31 offers a tremendous example of the service of the mouth versus the service of the heart:

> But what do you think? A man had two sons, and he came to the first and said, 'Son, go, work today in my vineyard.' [29]He answered and said, 'I will not,' but afterward he regretted it and went. [30]Then he came to the second and said likewise. And he answered and said, 'I go, sir,' but he did not go. [31]Which of the two did the will of his father?"They said to Him, "The first."Jesus said to them, "Assuredly, I say to you that tax collectors and harlots enter the kingdom of God before you.

This passage is relatively self-explanatory. The first son says no but repents and goes. The second son says yes and does not go. Jesus asks the chief priests and elders, "Which one did the will of the father?" Immediately, they knew to say the first one truly obeyed. If you are like me, you instantly knew that the first son, although initially rebellious, turned and obeyed the command of his father. The second son knew what to say, but when it came time to act as an expression of his heart, it was revealed that his walk did not align with his words. Lip service is not only a man-glorifying error, but it is also a deceptive and fatal condition of sin.

When God speaks to your heart, whether or not you obey His voice is not revealed with your lips; it is revealed with your life. Read verse 31 and ponder this question: Why did Jesus rebuke the elders and chief priests when they answered the question correctly? Because He knew their answers were head knowledge and not a reflection of their hearts.

Although it can be difficult at times to take a close look at your heart, ask yourself: Would God say to me what He spoke to these men? Am I man or woman guilty of honoring God with words when my heart is actually far from Him? That condition is very costly to the Body of Christ. It is a deceptive and subtle tool of the enemy.

Our society is saturated with youth, young adults, and adults who possess head knowledge of the Scriptures that would blow your mind. Although it is a positive thing to study and investigate the Word of God, there is no miraculous, authoritative power of God without application of that knowledge. Those Pharisees and priests that Jesus constantly rebuked held more knowledge of the Bible than you or I could ever hope to attain. Their problem was they got it with their heads but missed it with their hearts. If you miss it with your heart, then you don't have it at all.

Never forget that it is all about humble obedience to God. It does not matter how qualified or unqualified you feel. Walk as a follower of Christ and reveal obedience with action. In doing this, you will put yourself in position to be used greatly by the Lord. Jesus performed many miracles in the New Testament through the lives of very unskilled and unlearned people. The only aspect that makes you and me different from men and women like Matthew, Mark, John, Esther, Ruth, David, or Peter is radical obedience!

Being a spokesperson for your Savior is a beautiful and powerful ministry if you actively submit to His Word. Being a spokesperson for Jesus when your heart is far from Him is brutal and devastating to the name of Christ. Generations of Christians have suffered from this lip-service mentality, and until we break free from its bondage and begin living in sacrificial obedience to Christ, we will never see lasting revival. God is interested in seeing hearts transformed. When a heart is transformed, that life will be visibly, audibly, and emotionally different. Release whatever is blinding or hindering you from personally stepping into this. Pray and ask Jesus to help you become a man or woman consumed with and living a daily life that reflects Him alone.

Regardless of how long you have said no to our Heavenly

Father, there is always that opportunity to repent. This means stop, turn around, and run into His arms. Oftentimes, the enemy bombards us with our disobedience of the past seeking to hinder our obedience in the future. We cannot alter that which has already occurred. What matters most is our heart in this moment.

Do you want to live a vain and meaningless life of lip service? That lifestyle will only disappoint you and leave you ineffective to the Gospel call. If God reveals to you that your heart is far from Him, repent immediately. Run to Him for salvation, deliverance, and healing. If He only exists in your head but not your heart, then you do not have Him. Following Christ is strictly a heart condition.

This does not necessarily imply that if God reveals an area of lip service in your life that you are not born again. It simply means that He wants all of you, especially your heart. Do you desire to be a ground shaking servant of Jesus Christ? Submission of the heart is the only way. So true are the words of the old cliché: "actions speak louder than words." Of all the things you and I most likely remember from our past, events or actions probably lead the way.

Finally, consider the fact that the single greatest moment in the life of every Christian revolves around the heart of obedience of a man named Jesus who physically sacrificed His precious blood to redeem our souls. Christ could have just told us He loved us. But how much more powerful it was to see that blood drip down that cross just for you! Nothing can silence the action of Christ.

CHAPTER TEN
His First Order of Business

D o you realize the importance of your life as a member of the Body of Christ? Without you, the Body would not be as strong as it could potentially be. In an effort to become an effective servant in the Kingdom of God, it is critical that we daily submit to the leading and authority of our Lord.

We could all argue that it is a little painful at times when God exposes the deepest darkest areas of our hearts. As we seek to walk closer in intimacy with Jesus Christ, we must keep in mind who we are in Him. Viewing ourselves constantly in a negative and demeaning manner can generate apathy. The Lord Jesus Christ doesn't want us to be hindered by feelings of inability. He wants us to be confident in His ability through our lives.

This final chapter will emphasize the importance of ac-
complishing the Great Commission (God's command to
Christians to teach and lead others to salvation) through men
and women who love Jesus with all their hearts, minds, and
souls and detest the very
presence of sin. Why did I
mention sin? Because God
hates sin! Why? Consider
deeply this statement:
Our sin cost God His Son!

> HE WANTS US TO BE
> CONFIDENT IN HIS ABILITY
> THROUGH OUR LIVES.

As followers of Christ, it is crucial to constantly examine our
lives for undetected or concealed sin. God certainly desires to
use us mightily, but he cannot operate through vessels that
are contaminated with unrighteousness.

You may feel like that is the end of the road for you because you are not perfect. No one is! God does not expect
perfection. He expects a repentant heart that faithfully seeks
to become more like the Savior. If perfection were a qualifica-
tion, no person would be capable of being an instrument in
His hand.

Consider the life of David. Adultery, murder, and many
other troubles plagued his life. Yet, he was considered a man
after God's own heart. Why? He possessed a heart of repen-
tance. You and I, my friend, will not see perfection until we
are seated in Heaven. It's not about perfection; it's about re-
pentance and submission.

The enemy desires nothing more than to squelch the fire
that God desires to burn within you. As you surrender and
submit to His voice, do not be surprised to see the devil attack

you from other angles. He will try to make you feel unworthy and incapable of being used mightily by God. Rebuke that lie and faithfully commit the intents of your heart before the feet of Jesus. His number one purpose for life is found in Matthew 22:37: "You shall love the Lord your God with all your heart, with all your soul, and with all your mind." Love Him with every single ounce of who you are.

To fall in love with the Savior, we must seek Him, spend time with Him, and cling to His Word. Make no mistake about it, that is and should be our main focus as a Christian. As you and I fall more in love with Jesus Christ, we become positioned to be His obedient servants.

Having established that our sole priority as a follower of Jesus Christ is to fall more in love with Him with each passing moment, we can now discuss why we are here. We are here, as children of God, to reveal the glory and love of God through the blood of His Son Jesus Christ by the power of the Holy Spirit.

I want to share something the Lord revealed to me while I was riding down the road in my truck preparing for an Easter sunrise service. What happened to Jesus three days following His death on the cross? He rose again! What did He do following the resurrection? Did he ascend immediately into heaven? "No." Read Mark 16, Luke 24, and John 20. They all say that **HE APPEARED**. Jesus became the first person to reveal and display the glorious resurrection power of God. He became the first minister of the redemptive act of the cross.

Jesus could have ascended at the very moment of His resurrection, but He wanted Mary, the disciples, and many others to witness and experience the atonement that offered mankind reconciliation to the God of the universe. Christ's purpose on this earth was to be the sacrifice for the sins of this world. Upon conquering death, He stepped out and displayed the Gospel message with His life. **HE APPEARED.**

How encouraging this is to the life of every believer! Our primary purpose for existing on the earth is to reveal and display our intimate love relationship with God. What do you think went through the minds of the people, even His closest followers, as Jesus stepped forth as the risen Savior? They marveled at the mere sight of Him. Because Jesus Christ obeyed, the Father was greatly glorified.

That's right. Jesus Himself walked in humility and obedience to the will of the Father. Nothing about His life was easy or luxurious. In fact, the Scriptures make it clear that He was a man who experienced much sorrow, persecution, and pain. So if the very Son of God walked in this measure of obedience, what makes Christians today think we are exempt from such service?

Are we living our lives in such a way that every move and decision we make—according to the voice of God—displays His redemptive work and gift of salvation? In other words, do we operate daily as ministers of the Gospel of Jesus Christ? There is no greater responsibility on earth than walking daily to fulfill the Great Commission of Matthew 28:

> Go therefore and make disciples of all the nations,
> baptizing them in the name of the Father and of the

Son and of the Holy Spirit, teaching them to observe
all things that I have commanded you; and lo, I am
with you always, even to the end of the age. Amen.

—Matthew 28: 19-20

If we are obeying the Great Commission, we are telling others about Christ, leading them to be more intimate with Him, and baptizing them in the name of the Father, Son, and Holy Spirit.

To this world, you may not carry the title of minister or evangelist, but in the eyes of Almighty God, every person claiming the name of Christ as Savior has the responsibility of sharing the Gospel. People walking in full submission to the Father will effectively demonstrate the Gospel message for the entire world to see.

HE APPEARED! That statement means more and carries more significance than you or I may realize. Why? Think from the perspective of a person alive at the death of Christ. You have heard about a Savior for most of your life—from your studies of Scripture, from your family, etc—but it

> DO WE OPERATE DAILY AS MINISTERS OF THE GOSPEL OF JESUS CHRIST?

just seems too uncanny. Then, you hear that one claiming to be the Messiah suffered a death on a cross. At that point, you could remain a bit skeptical. But when you see that He has risen and stands right in front of you, you are convinced.

In His earthly ministry, Jesus spoke powerfully and pro-phetically regarding His death. The resurrection was indeed an affirmation!

He shed His blood to provide the sacrifice. He rose from the dead to conquer death. He appeared to offer revelation of that victory.

If you are reading this book and are an obedient follower of Jesus, it is or should be your heart-beating-passion to spread the Gospel everywhere your feet touch. If our number one goal of attending church is to have fellowship, we are missing the point. If our number one goal of Bible College is simply to have head knowledge of the Bible, we miss the point. If our number one goal in attending Bible studies is to be uplifted and encouraged, we miss the point. All those things are fine in context, but please understand that it is all about you if those are your goals.

Whether attending church or even reading this book, our number one goal should be to draw closer to Him so that we can effectively **APPEAR** to all men as an example of the risen Savior. How else will this world see and hear about the chance they have for complete redemption?

The Lord gave me an interesting analogy while I was thinking about this subject. Taking a short break from writing, I reached into my pocket and pulled out a sample fragrance card my wife had stuck in my pocket while we walked through a store. Although I think it smells terrible, it is a powerful object lesson.

On this small blank card is a sample smell of what a bottle of the perfume would offer. Despite the fact that it is very meager in comparison to the size and costs of the original source, it perfectly represents what a customer would receive if he or she chose this product. I can put my nose to this small sample and smell the exact fragrance that exists within the original container.

THERE IS ONE DISTINGUISHING FACTOR IN YOUR LIFE—THE PRESENCE OF THE LORD.

Wouldn't it be nice if we could simplify our walk with Christ to that degree? If in every area of our lives we could be S.O.S.—**S**amples **O**f the **S**avior—then we would humbly and effectively fulfill His plan for our lives through the submissive act of obedience. If we could only walk like He walked, talk like He talked, obey like He obeyed, and physically appear before man in the glory of the Father as He did following His resurrection, something would begin to shake.

As you finish reading this book, Christian, please understand that if you heed the call and commands as did our Savior, you will put yourself in position to experience the fullness of what God can do through a surrendered vessel. Worldwide, if God's people fully submitted, we would experience revival tomorrow. You and I do not have to wait until we lose everything before we run to Him. It is an honorable act to drop everything first and appear to both God and man as a child desperate to know the Father more!

In chapter 6 we referred to Moses and the rebellion of the children of Israel while God conversed with Moses concerning the details of the tabernacle. We spoke a lot about the presence of the Lord, but a Scripture of importance was left out at that time in order that this book might close with it.

Back to the book of Exodus chapter 33: Moses was meeting with God; the children of Israel were rebelling and making a golden calf. Moses was in desperation. He prayed in verse 15 that God would not move him unless the presence of the Lord carried him. That powerful stance should be daily applied by all followers of Christ. But verse 16 really puts it into perspective:

> "For how then can it be known that I have found favor in Your sight, I and Your people? Is it not by Your going with us, so that we, I and Your people, may be distinguished from all other people who are upon the face of the earth?"
>
> —Exodus 33:16 (NASB)

As humans, we seek many avenues that offer us distinction in the eyes of the world. We want something that sets us apart from everyone else. Some desire prominence, so they work and campaign for political achievements. Some desire fame, so they train hard or work hard to gain the spotlight. Some desire to be infamous, so they rob, steal, or kill. Some desire power, so they abuse and mislead those under them. As a Christian, you can wash yourself of any and all desires in your life to compare to or measure up to another.

The apostle Paul states:

> Yet indeed I also count all things loss for the excellence of the knowledge of Christ Jesus my Lord, for whom I have suffered the loss of all things, and count

them as rubbish, that I might gain Christ.
—Philippians 3:8

There is one distinguishing factor in your life—the presence of the Lord. Listen to what Moses asked: "Lord, without Your presence how will others see Your grace? Lord, without Your presence what will separate me from everyone else on the face of this earth?" Moses knew the distinguishing factor in his life was the presence of Almighty God. He knew that under the authority and leading of that presence there was a peace and power which could not be achieved in any other fashion.

> GOD'S ACTIVE PRESENCE IN YOUR LIFE WILL POSITION YOU FOR SPIRITUAL GREATNESS.

The presence of God is what sets you apart as a believer from everyone and everything else on earth. It is not a competitive thing within the Body of Christ but is equally available to all. You can stop seeking the favor and respect of man. You can stop relying on your own abilities to set you apart. God's active presence in your life will position you for spiritual greatness.

At a baseball tryout many years ago, I stepped onto the field looking to rise above all the rest. An honest assessment of my personal abilities revealed my skills adequate and equal to about a hundred other young, ambitious athletes. However, there were about three young men who obviously had a distinguishing talent. Whether it was exceptional speed or exceptional arm strength, there was visibly something special about the abilities they possessed, and I could see it. Because of those distinguishing factors, those men were asked to stay for batting practice while the rest of us were thanked and sent on our way with a handshake. I left disappointed.

Trying to be distinguished and measure up according to the terms and competitiveness of this world will leave you disappointed and heartbroken every time. In the presence of the Lord, there is never a competitive spirit or potential let down. God has a unique plan specifically designed for you.

No matter how great or small your ministry is, there is no need for competition because you contain the distinguishing factor: His presence. If you walk in His presence and lead a Sunday school class, you are distinguished because of Him in your life, not because of the size of your ministry or details of your vocation. If you are set apart because of a church size or a title on your door, then be prepared for imminent failure. If you are set apart by the power of God through the presence of the Lord in your life, get ready for miracles.

What is so distinguishing about His presence? It equips you to live a life which exemplifies the life of Jesus. In His presence and daily filled with His Spirit:

➢ You will walk in love and honor toward all those you meet.

➢ You will desire to love your Lord with all your heart, mind, and soul.

➤ You will desire to fulfill the Great Commission.

➤ You will desire to be a better husband to your wife.

➤ You will desire to be an obedient child to your parents.

➤ You will desire to operate with Him in mind instead of yourself.

By seeking, as Moses did, to walk humbly and obediently under the presence of the Lord, you will allow the character and love of God to form your identity. That is an identity that will set you apart and set your nation ablaze for the Gospel of Jesus Christ!

APPENDIX A
The Gospel Message

Within the pages of God's Word, we can read account after account of mighty miracles that occurred. They happened in the Old Testament; they happened in the New Testament; and they happen today. Oftentimes, we hear the term miracle and our minds gravitate to physical healing. That is certainly justified due to the fact that many of the miracles we read about within the life of Jesus Christ involved circumstances like the blind seeing, the deaf hearing, the lame walking, and the dead being raised to life. Those are miracles and powerful ones indeed.

Despite the potency of such acts, one miracle reigns supremely above any and all others and it is this: You and I have the opportunity to call upon the name of Jesus Christ and be, "…rescued from the dominion of darkness and brought into the kingdom of the Son he loves, in whom we have redemption, the forgiveness of sins" (Colossians 1:13-14).

Every person naturally carries the sin nature. With the fall of man in the Garden of Eden, fellowship with the Lord was broken and sin entered this world. That means that you and I were born with the same wickedness and imperfections that separate mankind from God. The only way we can erase the sin debt that grips our lives and destroys our fellowship with God is by calling on the name of Jesus Christ as Savior. In that way, the Lord, "called you into fellowship with his Son Jesus Christ our Lord" (1 Corinthians 1:9).

God sent His only begotten Son into this world to save us from the destruction our sin created. He paid the ultimate sacrifice by shedding His precious blood on the cross in our place that our sins might be forgiven. He was buried, and on the third day, He rose from the dead, proving His power over death and His ability to destroy the symbol and expression of our separation from God. Beautifully, the Word declares that He did this "…while we were still powerless" in order to "…demonstrate his own love for us" even though we were "God's enemies" because he wanted to restore fellowship with us. (Read Romans 5 and II Corinthians 5.)

The Bible makes it clear. If we confess with our mouths that Jesus is Lord and believe in our hearts that He paid our sin debt, then we will be eternally saved and granted a place in Heaven where we will forever be with the Lord.

> If you confess with your mouth the Lord
> Jesus and believe in your heart that God has
> raised Him from the dead, you will be saved.
> —Romans 10:9

Please do not take this lightly. Salvation is more than merely repeating a few words in prayer. Believing in Christ with your heart means the entire core of who you are experiences a life change. Confessing Jesus as Lord requires giving Him full authority over your life. When God takes over your life, everything about you will experience a renewing as you seek to be more like your Savior Jesus Christ. To be a Christian is to "be like Christ." Although we will never live perfectly as He did, we must seek to model our lives after His. He paid the ultimate price, and He did it for you.

If you cry out to Jesus today, call on Him to be your Lord and personal Savior, and mean it from the very core of your heart, then you can rest assured that He will save you from the chains and bondage of this world and hell. You will become an heir to the Kingdom of God.

WWW.SubMissionMinistries.ORG